# GRAND PRIX
## THE KILLER YEARS

# GRAND PRIX
## THE KILLER YEARS

JOHN L. MATTHEWS

**Press quotes from**
***Grand Prix: The Killer Years* the film and previous work**

'A documentary that will shock Lewis Hamilton to his very core'
*Time Out*

'Exemplary documentary'
*Radio Times*

'Tragic. Brilliant'
*Autosport*

'Terrific'
*The Guardian*

'A sobering, shocking documentary'
*Daily Telegraph*

'What a nightmare and what a fantastic film.
I cried out loud'
Victoria Parrott, *Autocar*

'An illuminating, moving film'
*The Observer*

'One of the best rallying documentaries ever'
*Top Gear*

This edition first published in Great Britain in 2016 by
ARENA SPORT
An imprint of Birlinn Limited
West Newington House
10 Newington Road
Edinburgh
EH9 1QS

www.arenasportbooks.co.uk

ISBN: 978-1-909715-41-7
eBook ISBN: 978-0-85790-905-3

First published in Great Britain in 2014 by
Bigger Picture Projects Ltd

Illustrations courtesy of and copyright © Paul 'Loudhead' Burnett
loudhead@uwclub.net

British Library Cataloguing-in-Publication Data
A catalogue record for this book is available on request from the
British Library.

Designed and typeset by Polaris Publishing, Edinburgh

Printed by Clays St Ives

# CONTENTS

ABOUT THE EDITOR                    XII

FOREWORD                           XV

INTRODUCTION                       XIX

ACKNOWLEDGEMENTS                   XXV


1   DAVID 'BEAKY' SIMS             1

2   SIR JACKIE STEWART            13

3   JACQUELINE BELTOISE           35

4   RENÉ BOVY                     47

5   JOHN SURTEES OBE              61

6   JEAN-PIERRE  BELTOISE         77

7   JACKY ICKX                    91

8   JACKIE OLIVER                105

9   NINA RINDT                   113

10  EMERSON FITTIPALDI           125

11  BEN HUISMAN                  139

12  JACQUI HAMILTON              149

To my brother Brent. Miss you.

# ABOUT THE EDITOR

JOHN L MATTHEWS first made a film when he was about ten years old around the dining room table, *The Death of Mr?*, filmed on a non-portable VHS video recorder. Having worked for his family's business for ten years he left with no A-levels with the idea of becoming a journalist.

He attended Durham University to study English, leaving to go to St John's College, York, having met someone at a party who was 'having a much more exciting time on a film course'. He studied TV, Drama, Literature and Film and in his last year won a Royal Television Student Award for creativity.

Whilst working part-time for BBC Radio Leeds he was one of four thousand applicants to reply to an advert in the *Guardian* for a researcher position at Granada TV's Factual Department. He was successful and worked on *What the Papers Say* and *University Challenge* on BBC 2, later *Dispatches* on Channel 4, where he learnt how to carry out large scale investigations.

Since setting up his own business, Bigger Picture Films, John and his team have been nominated for a Grierson Award for Best History Film for *Deadliest Crash, Grand Prix: The Killer Years* being long-listed for a BAFTA, winning the members' vote.

John is a keen motorcyclist and is happiest outdoors. This is his first book.

# FOREWORD
## from DAVID TREMAYNE

OF ALL THE MOTORSPORT films I've been involved with, none has elicited as much comment as producer John Matthews's *The Killer Years*. Part of that is because it was shown on television and on aeroplanes, but mostly that was due to the way in which he and his cameraman and co-director Richard Heap tackled their subject. This wasn't a big budget movie like *Rush*. It was two guys with passion and a dream touring Europe in a VW Combi, seeking to tell a story that they believed needed to be told.

The years from 1960 to 1976 were some of the sport's most glorious yet cruellest – a time when Jackie Stewart rated his chances of survival as one in three – when even that great fatalist Jacky Ickx remarked, "Survival is not a question of talent, but of luck."

I remember the chill I felt while writing *The Lost Generation* when, speaking of Roger Williamson's 1973 accident at Zandvoort, Jackie had said, "We drove through fire a lot in those days."

As Jacky Ickx said, drivers in those days were, "Young, with no fear and plenty of dreams. You go for it."

But what a price so many young men and their families paid in that era. Chris Bristow; Alan Stacey; Wolfgang von Trips; Ricardo Rodriguez; John Taylor; Lorenzo Bandini; Bob Anderson; Jim Clark; Mike Spence; Lodovico Scarfiotti; Jo Schlesser; Gerhard Mitter; Bruce McLaren; Piers Courage; Jochen Rindt; Ignazio Giunti; Pedro Rodriguez; Jo

Siffert; Jo Bonnier; Art Pollard; Roger Williamson; François Cevert; Peter Revson; Mark Donohue. And that isn't even the complete list.

The film is largely narrated by the men who survived: Stewart; Ickx; Tony Brooks; Jean-Pierre Beltoise; John Surtees; Emerson Fittipaldi; Jackie Oliver – with background from Nina Rindt; Jacqueline Beltoise; designer Len Terry; mechanic Dave Sims; the late writer Christopher Hilton and track representatives René Bovy and Ben Huisman. It's backed by a series of images which are, at times, brutal, as they capture an era in which the suppression of fear, and often – too often – minimal attention to safety were paramount. An era when teammates were obliged to borrow spanners to release stricken colleagues from crashed cars; when ambulance drivers got lost taking the injured away for medical assistance; when organisers and track owners frequently exhibited the most callous attitude to the men who took the risks which created the show in the first place. An era when those not close enough to understand the devastation wrought upon families and friends by each successive fatality chose to deify the fallen rather than to seek change to make the sport safer.

Had he not chosen the title that he did, Matthews might just as easily have borrowed a question posed by Stewart to name his film: What's the price of life? It stands as a graphic reminder of how things used to be, when tracks were grey ribbons threading through trees – and run-off areas lay far into F1's future. It's a shocking, hard-hitting story, yet a fine tribute to the heroes of a bygone era that shaped the sport into what it has become today.

And somehow the film – and now this moving book of transcriptions from its extensive interviews – resonates even more strongly in light of recent sad events at Suzuka during the Japanese GP on October 5th 2014, and the outcry from the self-appointed experts in the world of social media who have such little appreciation and understanding of the tremendous progress that has been made in safety in the intervening years.

DAVID TREMAYNE
Freelance motorsport writer and author of
*The Lost Generation*

# INTRODUCTION

MY FRIENDS DR MATT GIBBONS and Rich Heap have pestered me for years to bring a book out based on the films we have made. I've always been too busy making a new film and have never had the time. Or it's not felt right. Recently, however, an opportunity for such a book came about.

We have tried to make films about the most important motorsport stories – the ones that made people sit up and listen, that made changes, that improved the sport, that show what it is to be human. Therein lie stories of conflict and risk – of people struggling to do the right thing.

But when you make a film you end up only using about three per cent of all the material you spend several months – three years, in the case of *Deadliest Crash* – trying to find. And most of the material we find is amazing, so it's very difficult to decide which ninety-seven per cent to leave out.

That leaves almost all of the brilliant material on the cutting room floor. The question is: what do you do with it?

Here I share with you a big chunk of the ninety-seven per cent of the interviews we did *not* use when we made *Grand Prix: The Killer Years. Killer Years* was an obvious first book in this new series as it has been seen by millions all over the world, and it's the one film everybody seems to remember.

This is the original premise of the film, which also applies to this book:

*In the sixties and early seventies it was common for Grand Prix drivers to be killed racing: this was often televised for millions to see. Mechanical failure, lethal track design, fire and incompetence snuffed out dozens of young drivers. They had become almost expendable, as eager young wannabes queued up at the top teams' gates waiting to take their place.*

*This is the story of when Grand Prix was out of control. Featuring many famous drivers, including three times world champion Sir Jackie Stewart OBE, two times world champion Emerson Fittipaldi and John Surtees OBE, this exciting but shocking film explores how Grand Prix drivers grew sick of their closest friends being killed – and finally took control of their destiny.*

*After much waste of life, the prestigious Belgian and German Grands Prix would be boycotted, drivers insisting that safety be put first.*

*But it would be a long and painful time before anything would change. And a lot of talented young men would be cut down in their prime.*

*This is their story.*

Rereading these transcripts is utterly fascinating. They are so fresh and vivid: as interesting as when we first did the interviews – when we first wondered what to use in the film. You could take any part of these interviews at random, throw them together in any order, and it would make for fantastic and important reading.

However, I have not done that. I've gone through some of the most important parts of the interviews in light of the film's narrative and edited them together here, so that it adds to what has already been seen. The film is the starting point, as it puts these stories into context in a concise way [58 minutes 40 seconds, to be precise]. If you have not seen it you can buy it from www.killeryears.com. It includes never-broadcast extras. It would be a good idea to see the film before you read this book as it's a shock to see how lethal the sport had become. This book, rightly or wrongly, assumes you *have* seen the film.

One of our production rules is, 'Were you there?' All the people featured in the book have lost loved ones, close friends and family or been involved in key moments in an important way. The most heart-rending moments are such as those spoken by Nina Rindt and Jacqui Hamilton, talking of their last moments with their closest just before they are killed racing and the struggle to cope afterwards . . . how the world carries on regardless and how cruel that seems . . . how the bereaved are flown out of the place quickly. These stories are important, as these are the people left dealing with the loss for the rest of their lives.

Jacqueline Beltoise captures the thrill and the danger beautifully and knows more than most the pain that the out-of-control sport caused to so many. Her interview was not scheduled at all – we only asked her if she wouldn't mind doing it before we packed up from interviewing her husband Jean-Pierre. It is one of the most memorable interviews of them all. She lost her brother, François Cevert, in a race accident, on top of lots of her friends.

Interviewing Emerson Fittipaldi was a special moment in the whole of the *Killer Years* production. I remember his Latin warmth – his smile. He was talking of how – with all his friends being killed – he cried alone in his car in the car park, asking God if he should continue racing . . . of how he refused to race . . . and five people were killed the next day in that very race. As we parted he said, 'Thank you, John. That was the most amazing interview I have ever experienced.' I felt the same. If it had not been for Jochen Rindt's fatal accident, Emerson's career may have taken a very different path. Both Emerson and John Surtees also describe how perfect the relationship between man and machine can be.

And Sir Jackie Stewart – furious to this day about the death of Jimmy Clark and the loss of a host of other friends – describing his struggle to be heard about safety . . . and how, sometimes almost single-handedly, he banned Spa and other tracks from Grand Prix racing. Jackie was not entirely popular on his mission for safety and many disagreed with some of his ideas, like Jacky Ickx and John Surtees. John was a bike racer as well as a racer of cars and he saw things very differently. He also could see the weakness of the drivers' position – but, ultimately, Jackie Stewart's determination won the support he needed. Supporters like Jean-Pierre Beltoise explain the frustrations of losing so many friends, and he explains what has to be done to keep your focus. Beltoise won at the race where Clark was killed.

David 'Beaky' Sims reflects on what it was like being the last person to speak to Jim Clark before he died . . . the guilty feelings that remain to this day – and how he was just left to deal with the fallout – as a young man – on his own.

Jackie Oliver, promoted when Clark was killed, describes in vivid detail what it was like to narrowly avoid death in his Lotus . . . and Jacky Ickx explains the role of pure luck in it all.

René Bovy, general secretary of the doomed Spa-Francorchamps track, describes what it was like to be on the receiving end of Jackie Stewart's proposals – as does Ben Huisman, in charge at Zandvoort on the fateful day when Roger Williamson perished. René explains that making the changes which were demanded was not such a simple task as it may have appeared to the drivers.

When studying these fascinating interviews the problems

and complexities of the era are all too apparent: the book feels but an incomplete starting point on what remain the deep-rooted foundations on which the current Grand Prix is built.

These are real transcripts from real interviews.

When I interview I don't do what many do. I try to shut up and listen and I don't direct what is being said, nor do I fish for anything in particular – and I never put words in anyone's mouth. I allow the interviewee to tell his or her story. It's their story, not mine, so sometimes the stories can feel a bit disjointed. But if you transcribed any conversation you had today, it would probably not all make sense when you read it.

So please be understanding when things ebb and flow – or when they may seem to be grammatically incorrect, as what we have here are genuine recollections as they occurred: they are often from people speaking English as a second language and are transcribed directly from our film tapes, with only a little bit of editing here and there. An ellipsis denotes that the transcript may have been edited at that point.

What we have here is what was genuinely said. Imagine you are sitting next to the camera with your notes, listening intently, as I was lucky enough to do.

JOHN L MATTHEWS, director/producer of
*Grand Prix: The Killer Years*, Saddleworth, September 2014

# ACKNOWLEDGEMENTS

We have to thank Rich Heap for making these films with me, for helping prepare so thoroughly for the interviews and for helping make the place – full of cables, kit and cameras – as relaxing as it could be. And for using his incredible memory to stop my stupid mistakes.

Madelon, for helping find some of the most important footage.

Sarah Bagshaw, for beautifully translating the French interviews, and Sue Winger for typing every word into a transcription.

Glenda Hill-Wilson, for helping proofread and helping me at a difficult time, and of course for managing the whole production.

To Diana Horner from eBookPartnership.com and to Joanne Harrington at Written Proof for proofreading the final manuscript.

And to Janey, who edited the film and made it all into something special.

To H and to N for putting up with all my hard work and absences.

To Zoran, Martin, Mat and Bill for encouraging me through thick and thin.

To Richard K for commissioning it in the first place. This book, of course, could not have been made without those who kindly gave their time to be interviewed for our *Grand Prix: The Killer Years* film. I really want to thank the following for being so open with us:

Jacqueline Beltoise

Jacky Ickx

Jean-Pierre Beltoise

Jackie Oliver

René Bovy

Nina Rindt

Tony Brooks

David 'Beaky' Sims

Emerson Fittipaldi

Sir Jackie Stewart OBE

Jacqui Hamilton

John Surtees OBE

Chris Hilton, God rest his soul

Len Terry

Ben Huisman

David Tremayne

# 1

# DAVID 'BEAKY' SIMS

Jim Clark's mechanic at Lotus

Jim Clark Lowthird © 2014

*When you're the last person to talk to one of the world's best drivers – and I think he was – it still means a lot. Absolutely. It means a hell of a lot to me. And a lot of people ask me details and I don't normally tell them . . . not normally. But, you know, there is a point where people like yourselves think people should know. It should come out.*

I was Jimmy Clark's mechanic, and unfortunately I was his mechanic when he got killed at Hockenheim in 1968. I still feel that . . . and when you see books and pictures of Jimmy, and films . . . There were only the two of us, and we had just had a race in Barcelona. I had to drive from Barcelona to Hockenheim by the next weekend. He had an engine change and I had crash damage to do, and you are on your own.

He should have been at Brands Hatch but through some contract with . . . I think it was Gold Leaf, with Lotus, he had to be at Hockenheim with F2. Obviously the guy wouldn't be dead if he had gone to Brands Hatch, but he had to do the F2 race. It was a contract.

We worked two all-nighters in this garage underneath the hotel – Hotel Luxoff, by the river Rhine: still owned by the same people. I did the car. It was freezing cold that month. We got in the paddock – we had problems.

I don't think you could get a closer relationship regards

technical ability and knowledge and how to set a car up. I don't think there has ever been a combination that good because Jimmy had a way of calming and they would talk and have meetings and things would get done. Chapman respected that, and vice versa. Don't think there has been a partnership like that. Well . . . if there is, I don't know where. I don't know of a better relationship than those two guys.

He never got out of his tree: he was so cool, calm and collected, and he was a gentleman. He never swore – and away from racing, up in Scotland on his sheep farm, he loved to go and work with his sheep and his family. He just never got upset, and I think that is amazing.

He had unbelievable knowledge and feel for the car – his feedback what the car was doing. He had come to me – and we were only doing F2 testing – and he said to me, 'There is something wrong with the right front. It's picking up vibrations. It's got to be the right front.' So we checked everything. Nothing wrong with it. 'No, there's something there for sure.' So we got the car back to the base and stripped the front suspension both sides – and it was a wheel bearing going – a few notches in it. How had he felt that?

Special is an understatement . . . a unique person who never ever – a lot of drivers get angry, pissed off, frustrated, throw things about – I never ever saw him upset with people. Always cool, calm and collected – and he would go to Colin Chapman and say something about a problem and between them they would go and work it out and come back with a set-up sheet.

When you respect a guy like that . . . you'll work seven days a week all-nighters for a guy like that. Out of the car – in the car – he was amazing. If something went wrong with the car and that put him out of the practice session till the next day he would just say, 'Let's get it right. There must be something wrong because this did that with the engine: something is not working properly.' Then, you had to rely on the driver. Some drivers didn't have that ability, and you used to go up the wrong path on set-up and everything – but with Clark . . . Spot on. If he says it then you know you are doing it right.

Yeah, we had misfires – but that wasn't the cause of the accident like a lot of people think it was, because it wasn't that cold at the start of the race. He died on the seventh lap, I think. Jimmy said – on the grid, 'I don't like these tyres in these wet conditions.' It had stopped raining but it was still wet . . . not tropical wet, but it was wet . . . and then Hockenheim, a big long circuit – no Armco. Nothing. Just trees – and it was a fast, fast circuit. Jimmy said, 'Don't think I am going to go charging through . . . don't expect anything.'

Jimmy's last words were, 'Don't expect me to be up there in my usual position. I don't trust the tyres – I can't get no grip with them . . . can't get no heat in them.' He didn't like the tyres all weekend, hoping there was going to be a dry race – but it wasn't, and he wasn't happy with it at all. We adjusted the car, softened the shock absorbers – roll bars disconnected, to give it more grip. It was what he wanted, because he engineered the car. Not like now. There was not specific engineer data and all that stuff. He'd come in and say, 'It's understeering,' and, 'What can you do?' A couple of clicks later on the front shocks, and all that stuff. He actually engineered that car. He'd tell you what he wanted, and ninety-nine point nine per cent of the time he was smack on. He was very clever. I said, 'Good luck, and see you later.' As simple as that.

He started off and didn't come round, then a Porsche

driver came up and said, 'Can you come with me?' while the race was on. I saw the ambulance and I thought, 'Oh, dear' and then I thought, 'Where is the car? Where is Jimmy?'

This man said, 'Come with me,' and I saw what was left of the car. Where's the engine, where's the gearbox? Someone has taken it – I mean, what's going on? I started to get a little bit scared, and we found the engine and gearbox about fifty yards away in the trees. No seat belts, and Jimmy had been flung out of the car and hit his head on a tree. There were no seat belts in those days. It was about eleven or twelve feet high up in the tree where he got hit – and they wouldn't let me see, for obvious reasons.

I then asked the marshal guy, 'If you can radio Graham Hill and ask him to come in. I need help. What am I going to do?' Graham came in and we loaded the wreckage up. Graham was fantastic. He guided us through all that and he had to fly to where they took Jimmy, to say it was Jim Clark. They flew by helicopter and Graham didn't come back that night.

Colin Chapman arrived about 2 a.m. that morning – and you think, 'The world's best driver has just died.' So we loaded the wreckage up into the truck outside the hotel, and the police were guarding it. So we wouldn't leave, as it was an offence – probably still is an offence if the driver dies on the circuit – and Chapman says he wants it back. He says, 'I want you to leave now.' I said, 'What about the police?' He said, 'I don't care: I want it back in England. You got to go tonight. Drive.'

The police probably would have taken the car away and Team Lotus would never have been able to get it back, and you would not find out what had happened – what didn't happen – with the car. That's what happened in Italy with

Jochen Rindt. They kept the car. I think it was three or four years before Chapman got it back. They kept it, but this time we got it back.

We said, 'We can't.' He said, 'Yes, you can. You can do anything.' Luckily we looked out the window and the guy in the police car had driven off. So we just got our gear, jumped into the truck and we drove. We kept off the autobahns and we got to Belgium somewhere up near Spa, in the mountains. We found an unmanned crossing – it was borders then. And we lifted up the barrier and drove over and down this track – and, next thing, we were in Belgium, so we made for the port and we just made it to the boat.

We had tickets and they said, 'Jim Clark?' We said 'Yes.' They said, 'We want to take photographs.' We said 'No.' They said, 'No photographs, no boat.' So we had no choice but to let this sadistic guy take photographs of the wreckage – only of what we would show him – and he said, 'Okay. You're on the boat.' Then a policeman met us in England. They escorted us all the way home. We weren't allowed to go into the factory, and they parked outside – I think it was twenty-four or forty-eight hours. It was all stripped out. The engine went to Cosworth. The gearbox was sent to the manufacturers, to make sure nothing had seized in either. A lot of suspension parts went down to Farnborough, the aircraft place. Nothing was found to be wrong. The synopsis was that the tyres – there was an instant deflation – he was on a fast right-hander – just lost it, and went into the trees.

It was absolutely totally important to find out what went wrong. I mean . . . a lot of people will say he avoided the guy running across the track, which was nonsense. Others say that the misfire was the cause, which it definitely was not. The newspapers, then, the next day – I don't know which

9

paper it was. I can't remember. I have all the newspapers here, and it shows me bending down talking to him, and it's *Last minutes of Jim Clark's life* and it says *Mechanic left things loose* – and every paper had their own way of saying what went wrong with it, and it was all total rubbish.

I had come back and they told me to take two days off and I went back in and I thought, 'Well, do I carry on? Have I still got a job?' Then Chapman called me in and said, 'What do you want to do?' I said, 'I want to carry on.' He said, 'Right. Okay.' He said, 'I want you to take the spare car down to Barcelona in three days' time,' and he put me straight on to F1. He says, 'You have to get on with it. Life goes on. If you want to stay in motor racing you just have to get on with it.' All the team were really nice.

You never thought it would ever happen to him. It's impossible. He could never die – it's Jim Clark. Then it happened. That was a huge, huge reaction – a feeling in me. And a lot of other people, too. People knew him a lot better than I did – especially his F1 guys, who had been with him a long time, and the guys who worked on his Indycar [Indianapolis]. A lot of people were affected. I mean . . . I'm just one of many.

I think people suddenly realised that Jim Clark is not immune to getting hurt. People then start saying, 'Wow. If Jim Clark can get killed, I can get killed,' and that's why you hear of Jackie Stewart campaigning for safer cars and safer tracks, and he was a leader in that. Stewart did a good job. He was outspoken, but what Jackie did was positive and correct and he did show respect for the drivers – and people to this day respect that.

To start with you feel guilty that you were the mechanic and he died. But then, as the years go on . . . you did nothing wrong, and there was no blatant mistake made by any individual – and me, for certain. I was the mechanic. I was the only one working on the car. But to be associated with his death: that will go with me for the rest of my life. It will never go away, ever.

He is, to me, probably immortal. I'm still a big fan. I say that with feeling.

# 2

# JACKIE STEWART

Jackie Stewart *Lowdland* © 2014

*He is a Sir and an OBE but asked to be simply credited with his name.*

## ON JIM CLARK'S DEATH

I won the world championship in 69. Lost it in 70. Won it in 71. Lost it in 72. Won it in 73.

Sixty-eight had a big happening in that Jim Clark died on the seventh of April 1968, and he was undoubtedly the man to beat. If you were doing practice, testing, qualifying or racing, the question is, 'What's Jimmy doing?' You had to ask what Jim Clark's time was in comparison with what you might want to do – and every driver in the pit lane would have asked that question, as Jimmy was the natural leader.

Jim Clark died almost certainly by a vehicle failure of some kind. There was no barrier – no fencing – in front of a forest . . . and Jim Clark died violently in a forest, hit by young and big trees alike. His car was practically destroyed. The engine and the gearbox were gone and the car didn't exist, and Jimmy died.

Jim Clark never went off the road. He drove very smoothly and gently, and so why should he be killed in a racing car? It was inconceivable, and it woke up an awful lot of people.

When he died at Hockenheim motor racing was struck

for the first time by a hideous reality that death was to be our constant companion, because for four consecutive months that year a driver died. Jimmy, the seventh of April. Same weekend in May, Mick Spence died. Same weekend, one of the Ferrari drivers – and Jo Schlesser died at the French Grand Prix at Rouen.

I don't believe that anyone thought Jimmy could be killed. He was bulletproof in everybody's mind. I was doing a safety inspection at the Spanish circuit at Madrid when it happened. Someone came and told me he had had an accident and twenty minutes later he was dead. There was a race going on at Brands Hatch and when it was announced to the general public the whole place went silent.

It had an enormous effect on people that Jim Clark had died. The same has happened all through the years when other drivers have died. They are gone in a split second, and on many of those occasions we were on the track at the same time and had to go to the accident and to go to the driver – and if he was dead it was a very bad experience. It's deep and emotional and soul-destroying . . . and when it's something that should have been avoided . . .We were not at war. We were competing in a sport – almost a leisure-time sport, for public enjoyment. We would have been doing a great injustice to the sport not to have it changed as dramatically as it should have been.

I am angry, but not just about Jim Clark. I lost most of my friends. Helen and I counted fifty-seven people that had died that we knew well enough to call friends. What sport in the world do you know that could see that number of people being killed? A rebellion starts if there is more than one accident of that kind taking place in any one year, and it gets fixed these days. With the correct amount of authority and the correct amount of credentials you can get that done.

I had been trying for several years to get better safety within motor sport – and 68 was the turning point, because so many people died within a short time that the governing body of the sport at that time – who were trying to ignore the issue, the track owners – who were trying to avoid the issue, and a whole lot of the motoring writers – thought that drivers were gladiators, and were being paid for the risk rather than being paid for their skills as drivers. Suddenly I was getting through to the officials that they were required to significantly change their attitude towards safety – and, ironically, the fifth month of 68, the first weekend of August – the sixth and seventh – we were racing at the Nürburgring in Germany in torrential rain, in a race that should never have been started. Today that race would have been cancelled. The marshals couldn't see each other from one post to the next. A helicopter could not have landed.

## ON THE INCREASING DANGERS OF THE SIXTIES

Motor racing safety has changed enormously from the sixties to where we are today. It's like two different worlds. In those days we had an enormous amount of fires. A lot of people were burnt because the fuel tanks were just metal fuel tanks and the fuel was slurping along inside with a huge amount of vapour. If those fuel tanks were ruptured there would be an explosion because normally it's vapour that starts the fire, not the liquid. But then the liquid burns furiously and you have oil and rubber, all those things . . . We were having a number of people killed in racing accidents involving fire –

drivers trapped in cars because they were collapsing around the driver.

The sport wasn't out of control [but] it had developed itself beyond the physical elements of the track. Suddenly, coming into 1966, we changed from a one-point-five-litre car to a three-litre car. That's twice the engine size, which in some cases almost related to twice as fast. By the end of 68 going into 69 we had aerodynamics coming in, with wings – more downforce – therefore, higher cornering speeds.

During this time of increasing speed and doubling the grip of the car, plus braking efficiency, the tracks remained the same. There were no run-off areas; there were no deformable structures. If somebody hits a wall now in motor racing it is a deformable structure: the science and creation of the car today is designed and manufactured to collapse around the survival cell of the driver. The gearbox can come off, the engine can fly off, the wheels fly off – and the driver is left in a cocoon of safety, well strapped in and protected from whiplash ... Better seat belts, better crash helmets and better protection from the accident. The cockpit itself has fancy deformable rubber. When your knees crash into the side of the car – which is metal or fibreglass: composite carbon fibre – you could smash up your knees or your legs or ankles – but now you don't, because there is protection there.

No efficient marshalling could get them out of the cars in those days. If I were to take five years – from 68 to 73 – there was only a one out of three chance I was going to live. There was a two out of three chance I was going to die. That's a hideous batting average: never accepted by the governing body; never accepted by the track owners; never accepted by the medical staff. There were medical officers at every GP race, but they were not specialists in the field most needed. What you need is an anaesthetist to jump-start you. Mika Häkkinen was twice jump-started while he was still in a racing car because the people knew he was immediately in danger of dying and his heart stopped and they got it restarted because there were experts in that field. That wasn't happening in the sixties or early seventies.

## ON BEING RESCUED BY GRAHAM HILL AT THE BELGIAN GRAND PRIX, 1966

When I crashed at the Belgian GP in 66 we started the race in dry weather and it was around the Ardennes forest of Belgium, which is well known to be T-shirt and raincoat weather. One minute it's beautiful: next minute, it's raining. By the time we came to the fourth corner there was thunder and rain and seven of the best drivers in the world went off on the first corner. Aquaplaned off. I was not one of them. I had a bad start and came through and dodged all the traffic and the debris. There was a river of water and that's when you aquaplane.

Most cars can't handle the amount of water that was there that day, and I went off the road and hit a woodcutter's hut; knocked down a telegraph pole; hit part of a wall; went down into a lower basement area of a farmyard. I was knocked about and it was the first lap. The car was full of fuel and the tank had ruptured and fuel had come into the cockpit. The electrics were still switched on because the dashboard had been destroyed in the accident. Fortunately Graham came round and he had been slower getting through the debris, and he spun on the same river as I did. But there was nothing left to hit, as I had knocked it all down. Graham looked down and saw me from his car and could have continued, but came to help me – and in fact Graham borrowed spanners from spectators' cars to get the steering wheel removed to get me out of the car, as there were not removable steering wheels in those days.

I was stuck in the car for about thirty minutes and I was unconscious. I kept coming and going – they thought I had a back and pelvic injury. They finally got me out of the car and laid me in a hay truck and had to go and find somebody to go and get me an ambulance to come and get me. I don't know how long that took.

There was no communication in those days. It seemed that a big accident at the other end of the track was taking all their attention, so eventually I was taken back to a medical centre. I was on a stretcher and I remember being laid down on the floor and seeing cigarette ends on the floor in a medical centre. What they did to me I don't know. They put me in the back of the ambulance with two motorcycle police as escort. Jim Clark was in the back with my wife Helen and Stanley, who was running BRM. We took off and the police lost the ambulance and the ambulance didn't know how to get to the hospital. A comedy of errors: it would be a funny story if it wasn't serious. But when that happens to you, you realise that the system is way wrong and that no one seems to be looking after it. So we had an association called the GPDA [Grand Prix Drivers' Association] and it's still alive. We had by the early seventies an enormous amount of power to get safety put right, and it was mainly the GPDA that did that.

When I retired from racing I think the governing body said that that will never happen again; that the GPDA had too much power. To this day the drivers are being suppressed power-wise in respect to the influence they can have in the matter of safety. But what happened? The good news was that a man called Professor Watkins came along – and he was the man, if you like, that took over the baton from me. Mid to late seventies he started a big battle to put safety first in motor sport – and between the two of us, the sport today and . . . of course the gov- erning body took it up later on . . . But the risk management of F1 racing today is probably better than any industry or any sport in the world.

## ON CLOSING DOWN SPA

I went back to Spa and raced there the very next year and finished second or third, but we came to a point when we realised the track owners would not do what we requested – not even mildly contributing to doing it.

When any of the drivers – including myself – went back to Spa we were not warmly welcomed, because we were asking for money to be spent to take out barbed wire fencing designed to keep cows in fields rather than to keep racing drivers from hitting trees. So we were not a welcome sight even by the governing body, Belgium Motorsport. We wanted change. They didn't want change, because who was going to pay for it? The track owner had to pay for it . . . [so] We closed Spa and the Nürburgring, and that was a very serious thing to do. Nobody had ever done that before and I happened to be the president of the GPDA, so it was a very big decision. But the reason we had to close these tracks was the owners and representatives of the governing body responsible for Germany and Belgium just didn't want to listen.

They thought that they had more power than the drivers had. They thought they could make the drivers drive. Well, we didn't do that. We closed the tracks. Both tracks were in rural areas and the economy of that county was severely affected if there was no Grand Prix race going to be on. It was a very big decision to make and not one that we wanted to make. But if we were getting none of our requests accepted and just being told to go away . . . we were in a position where we have enough power – and because I was a world champion I was able to get [media] attention, but it was an uphill battle.

Safety didn't come easy and it didn't come cheap.


## THE GPDA MEETING THAT LED TO THE NÜRBURGRING BEING REMOVED FROM THE GRAND PRIX

The memorial service for Bruce McLaren took place in St Paul's Cathedral. Very big event, and we were all in attendance. After the service we went back to a suite at The Dorchester Hotel and we had a GPDA meeting. And we were all there. All the key guys were there, and we were going to go on about the Nürburgring. Jochen had gone there because he spoke German and asked for a whole list of things that we wanted them to do. At that time the Nürburgring was fourteen point seven miles around per lap: twenty-three kilometres; 187 corners. You took off thirteen times. Racing cars were not designed to fly: they didn't come down well. Always to be taking off, you had to be going fast – so when you came down it was a real hassle. A number of accidents could have happened, so we said, 'Unless they do the work that we ask for we will not race at the Ring.'

This was sacrilege. This was the temple – the most challenging race track in the world – and we are suggesting that we might close it down. So there was a lot of concern about that. But I said, 'We have to do it – because if we race there we have to race everywhere else, because these other tracks are not nearly as dangerous as the Ring. So why should we give preference to them and demand that lesser tracks do the same?'

If they won't do anything we cannot race. There was division in the ranks and I genuinely felt that we might lose it. If we had lost the vote – if there had been a majority of drivers who said we must race at the Nürburgring – I would have had to resign as chairman of the GPDA as I would not have agreed with them, and I would not have driven myself.

And Jack Brabham ... who was at the time the most senior member of the GPDA and a thoroughly experienced racing driver – who had already won the world championships a couple of times. He was very quiet and never spoke out on anything. He said, 'We have to go with Jackie. We can't go to the Ring. Look at the number of people who have been killed.' In that week we had services for Piers Courage *and* Bruce McLaren and here we were going back to the Nürburgring after they had said they would do *nothing* that we had asked. They were just holding a pistol to our head and thinking that we couldn't do it to the Nürburgring. The vote went in our favour and we did not race at the Ring. We went to Hockenheim instead. It was an awful loss to that region of Germany, but ... because the track owners would not go and spend money.

They then did of course [make the changes] and we went back in 71 and I won the race again.

In any confrontation of that level some of the drivers had more power than others. If you were a top driver you said what you wanted to say and you would get it to happen. Your team would get it done for you. Some of the drivers who were not having the same amount of success were considerably more vulnerable. 'If you don't race we will sack you,' so that was their livelihood going. Drivers' careers were on the line and so they had pressure on them that might have forced them to vote the other way. But in the end credibility is everything and you can't duck a reality and you have to stand up and be counted, and that's what happened.

It was a decision well made, and a decision that turned the Nürburgring around. It was later written off from motor racing after the Niki Lauda accident because no one could get to Niki in time. He did die and then was jump-started, but the fact was . . . That track could not be marshalled on both sides for fire – or for getting drivers out, or for getting doctors and ambulances to people – because there is twenty-three kilometres – that's forty-six, using both sides of the roads – and you couldn't get to some places because of ravines and forests. So, certainly, it was the right decision to be made – but not a popular one.

## ON THE CHALLENGE OF CHANGING THE CULTURE OF THE SPORT

What's the price of life? What price do you put on a man or a woman's life? . . . Because we were not just talking about the drivers themselves: we were talking about the spectators' protection. We were talking about a car that could reach the spectators and we were trying to avoid the type of accident that happened at Le Mans, where eighty-two people died [eighty-three spectators and driver Pierre Levegh died]. Or Monza, where von Trips went into the crowd and many people died. We didn't think the sport could afford that – never mind the life of drivers – because for some reason people were prepared to think that racing drivers were gladiators and accept that to go into the coliseum you had to expect to die. Well, I never thought that I was being paid for the risks I was prepared to take. I thought Jackie Stewart was being paid more than some other people because of the skills he had. Maybe they thought I was prepared to go blindly into some idiotic risk. That would be totally unprofessional, and none of us ever did.

I still have the hate letters to this day that say, 'Why don't you take your money and go back and live in Switzerland and give us a rest. Don't come motor racing.' A lot of people were negative about [safety] because they thought we were spoiling motor sport. There were no barriers in front of the pits, for example, so a car in Monte Carlo or anywhere else could have piled into the pits where there was fuel and high-ranking people in the sport. So if a car had done that it would have wiped out half of the hierarchy of motor sport. It was common sense not to allow that to happen – to put a barrier up to stop that possibility. Put up debris fencing just in case a wheel or a suspension unit flies into people and kills them. It was just not recognised by the people at that time that these things could happen. From a racing driver's point of view we could see what the trajectory would be if we got it wrong or if a mechanical failure occurred.

The critics would have been saying that I was chicken – if the kitchen was too hot why did I not get out? I was a professional racing driver and thought what I was doing I did quite well – and I did do well. It wasn't the money: it was the fact I loved the sport. But I don't think the sport had any legs on it the way it was going. I think eventually if a car had gone into the crowd and a lot of people got killed that might have ended the sport.

My responsibility was to myself and my family and to my fellow drivers as president of the GPDA. I was doing it for them and the long-term stability of the sport. The critics . . . I didn't laugh at them but for me I just thought they didn't know any better, so I was just sorry for them if they were that stupid that they would allow people like Jim Clark to die and all the other drivers to die. They had not been to the site of the accident of Piers Courage. They had never seen that, and if you have never seen death . . . it's something to avoid.

I have seen things that I would wish no other people to see, and they should not see it – and when you see the grief that is brought to the immediate family and friends – and you are going out to do the same thing – you have to have an amount of extreme focus to be able to go and do that. And for anyone to call me chicken – I was still winning Grands Prix and world championships, so I didn't have a lot of time for these people. I have no regrets for being so ardent in the steps that I wanted to take and the support I was being given by my fellow drivers, because a few people in the GPDA were arguing with that philosophy.

Some of them were being given incredible pressure to disagree and go and race, as this is our business as well. We could only do it if we were seeing improvements for safety to secure the long-term benefit of the sport. Today F1 is the biggest TV sport in the world. Bigger than the Super Bowl: bigger than anything else on an annual basis. Every year our numbers are higher and if you did a four-year average our figures would still be higher and that's because the sport is loved and we want it safe. It is safer now than it's ever been in the history of the sport, so those critics must look back . . . and I would venture to suggest that they might admit that they were wrong.

## ON JOCHEN RINDT BEING KILLED

Jochen was dead, I believe, by the time I got to him – and his last rites had not been read to him by the priest, but they did so when I was there. He had already been brought from the accident to the medical centre, which was quite primitive in those days. In Italy . . . Italian law . . . and I am not sure it's not the same today that if a driver dies under these circumstances the event would be cancelled, so Jochen was put in an ambulance and taken to Milan and he was announced dead on arrival. But Jochen was not alive at the track.

When Jochen Rindt died at Monza I had to go back out and qualify, and he was one of my best friends. He lived near my home and his wife was there and my wife was with her in the ambulance. He had already died and they didn't know it. These sorts of things you never forget. But if I am going to drive the car and qualify in it, then I have to wash these things out of my mind . . . I admit when I went out in that car I cried on the way out because I was so disturbed, because I had been with Jochen.

I got the deal done. I did three laps and I put myself into second on the grid, and when I got out the car I burst into tears again because the emotion is so deep: because you are travelling companions. You stay together in the same hotel . . . and going to the same restaurants. In those days the camaraderie was tight. You were living with each other a lot – going on holidays together. Nina, Jochen, Jimmy and

I went to the Bahamas to have a holiday together. Two years later two of them are dead. They had long-time partners and family who grew up with [my sons] Paul and Mark. So when you see that type of destruction in front of your very eyes it lives with you for the rest of your life.

And that is why I am still angry and emotional about it and nobody can forget it. You can push it aside from time to time but you never forget it, and that was a bad period in motor sport in respect of those who died. The sport still lives on today because it's still so violent, but people are surviving the accidents . . . It's an example to other sports – how you can manage risk and eliminate the unnecessary challenges and remove the downside risks – and that way the sport continues in a healthy and prosperous fashion.

Jochen was one of my best friends. I think in the period that I raced it might have been very similar to World War Two when fighter pilots were all mucking in together all in the same compound laughing and crying together, as they were losing each other from time to time. Somebody would not come back, but the world didn't stop. They still had to go back up and defend their country. We were not doing that: we were participating in a professional sport. But nevertheless I think it's that kind of mentality of the people of that time. And I think you can look at different arenas – in wars, particularly – where people are dying on a regular basis, but they still go on their tour of duty to do their work because they are professional people.

Jochen died in Monza in September. He was thinking about retirement. We had had the conversations about stopping being a driver and that year he was dominant. It was 1970 and he had the Lotus 49, which was fantastic. That was the year I was driving the March – so no competitor to him – but we were still close together and we talked about it, and I think he might have retired there and then . . . but he was so far ahead that there was still a chance that either I or Jacky Ickx could still win the championship. But – thank God – we didn't. My car wasn't quick enough and Jacky had a mechanical failure or something and he would not have had enough points to secure the championship in what was left of the title races.

So Jochen became the first ever posthumous world champion. Helen and I went to the presentation in Paris and Nina very bravely picked it up [the trophy] and behaved fantastically – and it's the first time it's ever happened in racing, and I hope it will be the last.

## ON QUITTING THE SPORT

There was more than once when I thought I would never drive racing cars again, but – ironically – it was never at a time that involved death or a serious accident. It was at a time when I got myself so low just through – I guess – overwork, or too much stress, or doing too many races or I was just run down. I could have retired at the end of 71, being the world champion – and feeling like I was. But I got out of it and in 72 I had the ulcer haemorrhage and . . . I could have easily retired at that time. I didn't think I was ready for retirement, and when in 73 I suddenly realised early in the season that I should retire – this is a clear decision, and I knew I was making the right decision . . . but I said I would race to the end of the season because Ken Tyrrell was relying on my participation.

So I told him I was going to retire, but I would race until

the end of the season. I didn't tell my wife. I only told three people. Ken Tyrrell was one of them and it was almost a help because I knew it was the last time that I would be in Monaco and it was the last time I would race an F1 at Silverstone – and therefore I got more pleasure and satisfaction because I knew I was not going to do it again. And when you know that, you have a higher sense of the real quality that the sport has given you.

In the end my last race, which should have been my one hundredth GP at Watkins Glen . . . and François [Cevert] was killed the day before in qualifying – and of course I knew that I was going to be retiring at the end of the next day. I had organised it so completely. Ford had organised a dinner for me in London. We knew the date: it was going to be my one hundredth GP, and I was the champion. At 11 a.m. in the morning François had this huge accident and we were all on the track and we all had to go to him, because we thought we were there first.

There was so much debris around him, so much confusion – and when you see someone in that condition and then you have to get into your car and drive back to the race track, it's not just sadness. You are angry. You are shocked that the sport could be as bad as it is . . . as negative as this . . . to have such violence as this.

I chose not to race the next day and it was a joint decision between Ken and I that out of respect for François we would not do that race. I may have won that race because everything was good. I drove after that: I drove the afternoon François died, because some of the mechanics had been afraid it was a mechanical failure and that would have been terrible for them. I was sure it was a human error, so I drove in the afternoon. I know exactly what happened to François and I did what I had to do – and that was the last time I drove a racing car in anger, if you like.

But it was a disappointing way for it to end, because it was as if God has said, 'You have had a fantastic life. You've got it: you've retired. You will live the rest of the season to win the world championship.' . . . I'm arranging the dinner with Ford, arranging a press conference to announce the retirement – and it was like a slap on the wrist, saying, 'You're not in charge. Don't take anything for granted.' It was a real wake-up call – but it would have been a fantastic thing to have seen François go on, as I think he would have won the world championship.

*The interview ended with a description of the inside of Ken Tyrrell's garage . . .*

# 3
# JACQUELINE BELTOISE

*This is such an evocative interview of its time that it has been left virtually uncut. Jacqueline captures beautifully the close-knit 'family' of the racers and their wives. And the ever-present horror and loss. It is a translation from the original French.*

It wasn't a brutal sport. Selfish, yes. Egocentric, even. Very selfish. Everyone was sad, certainly.

So many are dead now. I have a photo taken in 1968 or 1970. There are twenty-five drivers, and five of them are still alive. When I saw the photo I counted them – and there's Brabham still left; Jackie; Jean-Pierre; Jacky Ickx . . . and the fifth one . . . I can't remember who it was, but there were five left out of twenty-five. So in ten years – eleven years – twenty of them were dead.

It was not like nowadays, where they are too professional . . . back then, it was like being in a family that travelled around. We went in the same planes, in the same hotels. We had our meals together. We knew each other well: the women, the men. We were all really good friends.

Of course, on race days it was war – every man for himself – but the wives got on well together. I was very good friends with Helen Stewart, Nina Rindt. We were close. We confided in each other, not like it is nowadays. We followed our husbands everywhere. There wasn't a group of us, as such:

we were just with our husbands – but when they weren't racing we would chat together at the hotel. We'd have a drink . . . a very nice friendly atmosphere between the drivers and the drivers' wives. Everyone got on well.

And it was great when we went abroad, when we took the plane. The sponsors and the constructors – they chartered a flight. There were the journalists, the sponsors, the drivers, the mechanics, all the drivers' wives – even Moët et Chandon. The plane was especially for the race. Everyone was there. It was great. We had a good time in the plane.

It's changed now. Now every driver has their own plane. They don't talk to each other. They don't know each other. Before, everyone knew everyone else. As soon as there was a problem people went to help. Whenever there was an accident everyone hurried over to see if the driver was injured – if it was serious. I liked Barcelona, a favourite circuit. I liked that a lot – the old one, of course. I was never in the stands. I didn't keep the times: I didn't like that. I filmed it.

For instance, when we used to go to Monza we went down to the Villa d'Este. We went with our children. I remember my son Antony was about fourteen or fifteen months old. François [Cevert] my brother was there; Jackie was there with Helen and their kids. François would be playing with the kids – with my son – in the swimming pool. Everyone was there. And then suddenly my son started to walk. They were the first steps he took, and everyone clapped – all our friends – the drivers. It was so nice. Really wonderful. I loved that time in our lives.

What was sad was that there were maybe two or three deaths every year. That was very difficult.

I can tell you about Hockenheim, to tell you how it was when Jim Clark was killed. We had come in a Mercedes.

At that time we travelled in cars. We didn't take planes or helicopters: that didn't exist. We travelled to the circuits by car – to Monza, Spa, everywhere, by car.

We were very sad. The first death I experienced I had just got married – in 68 – and we were there for a Formula Two race – and Jim Clark, who we already knew well, came up to me, gave me a kiss and said, 'It's great. We're so happy you and Jean-Pierre got married.' Graham [Hill] – who was his teammate – gave me a kiss as well, and then at the race, Jim set off . . . and it was over. It was terrible. Terrible. Jean-Pierre won that race, and on the podium he was crying. Everyone was crying. On the podium he won, but he was crying. I've still got the photo.

We had a dog at that time, called Enna – we had one dog called Monza and one called Enna . . . We used to take Enna everywhere with us, ever since she was a puppy. She came with us to every track. She was an extraordinarily kind dog. Everyone knew her. We would leave the car open and she'd guard the car: she wasn't on a leash. Or she'd even sleep in the stands with all the exhaust fumes, which didn't seem to bother her at all. And when Jim got killed she must have sensed it. She just didn't move. She was completely transfixed. Normally when we came up she would be all happy, wagging her tail – and this time she just looked at us, completely still.

She got into the car, and we had trained her to lie down on the floor in front of the seats – and I'd rest my feet there, and she'd move around a bit, but this time she didn't move at all for the whole journey. She had her head right next to the gearstick and was just looking at Jean-Pierre. It was incredible. She knew that something awful had happened. And in the car Jean-Pierre was crying at the wheel, too. I just remember that now. It's funny how this dog had sensed everybody's sadness:

she was traumatised, too. Everyone used to pat her and stroke her; she's in all the photos. She's dead now, but she came to every race with us until she died.

I hadn't yet realised that it would happen again. I thought it was a one-off; it wouldn't happen again. And then two months afterwards, Jo Schlesser got killed. And then, every year, something serious happened. After Jim's death I was sure that it wouldn't happen again. That it was over: that no one else would get killed. I was young. I didn't realise it was so dangerous; I didn't know it was dangerous.

I remember the accidents when I was there, yes. Jo Schlesser also, who was French . . . That was in June in 1968 at the French Grand Prix in Rouen. He was very skilful; he lived really close to us in Neuilly. He was a friend – a very good friend – and that was awful, too.

After Jo's death, Jo Schlesser . . . It was horrible. The car exploded. It caught fire in the descent towards the corner; the car just plunged straight on. It was a mechanical problem. Jean-Pierre said at the time that when a driver gets killed it's down to a mechanical problem. I saw Jo coming, and then I saw the accident. It was terrifying. There was petrol all over the track and the cars were driving on through the flames. They didn't stop the race. It was horrifying. I didn't think that cars could pass through the flames. Rindt stopped to change his tyres because they had caught alight. In those days they didn't stop the race.

But then, every time it's awful – and it's hard to say, but . . . At the beginning, I was shocked. I was young: I was 22 years old. I was discovering racing. I was fascinated by it because of my brother François, who introduced me to it when we were very young. And there is one, two, three, four, five deaths. And you're very sad and very unhappy, but then in the end –

it's terrible what I'm about to say – you get used to it.

You get used to the fact that someone is going to kill themselves. You always think it will never be one of your own. I always thought that nothing would ever happen to either Jean-Pierre or François. Helen [Stewart] thought the same thing. Every one of us thought it was something that never happens to you. So then it was Jo Schlesser, which was terrible, and then Courage, who was a very good friend. And then after that – the worst, of course – it was François.

In the end – with hindsight – it was normal, when you think about it. When you see now how it was during those years, it was only natural that so many people got killed. The cars were not strong. The petrol tanks – as soon as there was an impact the tanks caught fire . . . Not like it is now.

They were very difficult times for the drivers – for everyone – and yet at the same time they were years of camaraderie, friendship, fun. It was very friendly. Off the track it was like a travelling circus. There were two sides to it: the tragic side and the loyal, friendly side. I've stayed great friends with Jacky Ickx. He called me when he was at Le Mans only a few days ago. We see each other in Monaco.

I know that Helen was very traumatised. She was very afraid. She was much more aware than I was of the danger. I wasn't aware. When you're in the stands you keep time – you're waiting, and you see that he's late. Immediately you think something must have happened. If he's not on time, he's come off the track. Something's wrong.

Whereas I was on the track: I had my camera, and I just didn't realise the danger. My passion was filming the race – cars overtaking. I was fascinated by that, and I couldn't imagine the extent of the danger at the time at all. And at each race I was in the grip of that passion for the race itself, and for the filming of it. The only time I was in the stands it was at Monaco, when Jean-Pierre won the Monaco Grand Prix in 72. It was raining hard so I went in the stands and I had my chronometer, and when Jean-Pierre went past on the first lap I just dropped it. I dropped it and closed my eyes and was thinking, 'That's it. He's going to go off the track. He's going to have an accident,' for the whole seventy-five laps. I had a friend next to me who told me when he had gone past. I was so afraid there was going to be an accident. When you're in the stands, you're afraid. Nowadays there are computers, but back in those days it was the drivers' wives who did the timekeeping. It was different.

I was afraid only one time for Jean-Pierre. Very afraid. It was at Jarama, in Madrid. It was a Formula Two race, and I had gone up on to the roof of the stand – and suddenly I saw a crash. I recognised Jacky Ickx's Ferrari. There was a fire – it exploded – and I looked for Jean- Pierre. And I didn't see him come past. I said to myself, 'Jacky and Jean-Pierre have crashed.' I was so afraid, and I looked at the home straight because I was in the stands, so I filmed the accident at the corner opposite, and then looked at the finish line – and when I turned Jean-Pierre had already gone by. So I was convinced he was involved in the crash with Jacky Ickx. And then the next lap I spotted him. But for a whole lap I thought he was the one in the accident with Jacky. Jacky was burnt on his buttocks. On his legs.

In Rouen it was fabulous. All the drivers were introduced to the crowd before the race, and each one was in a convertible car. And I was down at the Nouveau Monde, at the edge of the track. And I was filming, and they were doing this – blowing kisses – all of them. All of them. They were so used to seeing me filming that they always used to wave and say 'Hello.' Even Jo Schlesser, who was killed at that track: he stopped his car and he came to talk to me. I can't remember what he said now – something like, 'Hey, sweetie. Get some good shots,' and then he started up the car again and drove off. All the drivers ... there was not one who didn't say 'Hello' to me. But that's because between the races – or before the race, or after the race – we all dined together; we celebrated together.

At each race Graham [Hill] made extraordinary speeches. He had a fantastic sense of humour. He'd describe the race in his own way – I can't tell you – but Jean-Pierre would be there, and everyone was laughing. It was great. Rindt as well. He paid a special tribute: I remember it was at Clermont-Ferrand. It made everyone very happy. Now there wouldn't be a driver who would do that. When I look back at that time I think the drivers were so honest, sincere – and they recognised the value of the others. Nowadays they are constantly at war with each other.

At the French Grand Prix – I can't remember what year it was – Jean-Pierre was in the Matra, and Rindt was in another car – I can't remember – and Jean-Pierre set off ahead. He was very far up in front, very far ahead, and he got a puncture – a slow puncture, you know? So suddenly he almost came off the track, and it was one of his friends at one of the corners who signalled to him there was a problem. So Jean-Pierre had to stop and change the wheel. The race was over for him. He set off again, but it was over. He finished sixth or seventh – something like that. And it was Rindt who won – who had been in second place. He won the race. And as Rindt had to do a speech at the end – there was a prize-giving and a dinner afterwards – and at the prize-giving Rindt got his trophy and he said, 'It's not me who won. It's

Jean-Pierre who should have won. I would never have won if Jean-Pierre hadn't had a puncture.' It's lovely that he said that. 'I could never have caught him up,' he said. It was a lovely speech, a really beautiful tribute to Jean-Pierre.

I realised that Jean-Pierre had a ritual that helped him relax before a race. He was so stressed the night before a race that I realised afterwards that's what it was, but the first time it was a shock for me. We were at the dinner table. I remember the first time it was in Pau. My brother François was racing in Formula Three, and Jean-Pierre in Formula Two. So we were all at the dinner table – even François was there with his fiancée – and there was Lagardère, and the mechanics and the engineers were there too. Jean-Pierre must have been opposite me, I think, and we were eating – and then, when we got to the cheese course, suddenly Jean-Pierre hits the table and says, 'There you are. She's annoyed me. What's it to do with her? . . .' He started saying all these angry words about me. 'I can't take it any more. I've had enough.' And he gets up and leaves and walks out of the restaurant. I was terrified.

I just sat totally still, and there was total silence. And then Lagardère was saying, 'Come on, everyone. Eat up,' and the dinner continued. But afterwards I knew I had to go upstairs to the bedroom. So I go in, really quietly, and he's asleep. So I get into bed. The next morning he wakes up – 'Morning, darling,' – and I couldn't understand it. He'd forgotten it all. And he did this to me before every race for eight years.

He would wake up in the morning in perfectly good spirits, after having thrown a tantrum at me. He let it out on me, and I had never done anything wrong. If one day you see Pescarolo, he would laugh – because we always used to have dinner with Henri.We practically lived with Henri for almost ten years because he was racing in Formula One, and then in the prototypes with Matra – so we would often spend time with Henri Pescarolo.

And Henri would laugh and say, 'There we go. That's it: he's having his tantrum again.' He'd say, 'Bravo. Well done.' It made him laugh like that because it had become a ritual. Jean-Pierre had to let himself go and take out all his stress on me – and then the next morning all was well. He'd be relaxed at the track, not stressed at all. And I'd be totally fed up with it. I'd be in a panic every time because I didn't know what I'd done or said – nothing.

# 4
# RENÉ BOVY

*René had been in charge of Spa-Francorchamps since 1946. In the 1960s he became the general secretary of the track: his job involved preparing the circuit for Grand Prix races. In this capacity he met Jackie Stewart – the culmination being that Spa was removed from Grand Prix, something nobody expected. It is interesting because he explains the problems of this period from the side of the track manager, dealing with fatalities, etc. You can see where Jackie Stewart and others' frustration stemmed from. René was eighty-eight years old when he did this interview. It is translated from the French.*

In the 1960s safety measures were almost non-existent. There were no crash barriers, which meant that cars left the track and flew off into the countryside. There was nothing there to stop them. Safety measures were not like nowadays, where there are one, two, three barriers . . . preventing the cars from coming off the road.

At that time, the Spa-Francorchamps track was right in the middle of the countryside, in woods and meadows. There was the plot where the track was, and fences – smaller 'chicken fences' to distinguish between properties . . . meadows, the woods, villages. So there was nothing to keep the cars on the track in the event of an accident, from 1960 to about 1970.

It's in a wild, natural landscape, with forests, woods and fields. It's totally pure, not like a track through the streets of a town like in Monaco. It's right in the middle of nature . . . We would close the circuit off for the race, but outside of that it was a normal road. It's an open-road circuit. Now it's a proper track but then it was a circuit of closed public roads, used for normal driving outside of the race.

We were proud because, at that time – along with Silverstone and Monza – it was one of the fastest tracks in Europe. For example, at Francorchamps on the home straight you could reach up to 360 kilometres per hour. That's one hundred metres a second: it's very fast. And that's because the home stretch at Francorchamps is downhill. Here, it's extraordinary. It goes uphill, downhill – there are flat open straights, there are corners. It's very natural . . . I think for the drivers it's one of their favourite circuits.

In general, even if it's raining, we still start the race.

## ON 1966 AND FATAL ACCIDENTS

It was a terrible year because there was a corner where they all crashed into each other and two of them were killed. It was one of the most serious accidents in Formula One. I think it was in 1966.

It was very difficult because I was also secretary of the town council at the time, so I had to do the death certificates and I had to do an inventory of the drivers' belongings – what they had on them. We took them to the infirmary – to the emergency station – but they were both already dead. Chris Bristow had been cut by a wire – an iron wire from a fence.

I wasn't the race organiser. I was organising the whole

show: the track, the facilities – and, also, I was in charge of the accidents. So I had to organise the ambulances, go and get the bodies and bring them back to the morgue. There I had to do the inventory of their papers, what they had on them – and after that – if there was family – I had to get them over there, to contact them. It was painful, difficult . . . because you are dealing with people who are in pain because of a catastrophe; because of the death of a loved one.

These are events that are always difficult, because they are tragedies – for the team, for the families, for everyone. And then you have to take care of the transfer of the bodies – the dead – back to Great Britain. That's when I met that guy who made the Lotus, Colin Chapman. I was in touch with him to arrange the repatriation of the two that were killed [Stacey and Bristow]. One was in a Lotus and the other was in a Cooper. So we got the bodies back to England from Brussels.

It was very serious, but one must point out that those two drivers had always raced in England on flat tracks like Silverstone – a former airfield – and when they came to Belgium they were racing on an open-road track. Much more turbulent, with corners that went uphill and downhill – and it didn't agree with them. They didn't have experience of that sort of circuit.

I can tell you that certain drivers who are not top-rate, extraordinary ones . . . in the rain, sometimes they reveal themselves to be great drivers. Very good drivers. Sometimes there are champions who are not very good when it's raining. But others, the less important ones, they go for it and they win races. That's happened several times.

I'll show you later the place where Stewart went off the old track. I should say that there were incidents related to Stewart's accident. He missed the Masta Kink, and he plunged down below into a farm. And he was injured. And the ambulance took twenty minutes to come to his rescue. We don't know why the ambulance took so long.

His car was totally demolished. I'll show you the photo. You have to see that: I can't explain it. But you'll see it on the photo. I've got it to show you, especially.

## ON JACKIE STEWART

The first meeting I had with Jackie Stewart was at prac- tice on the Friday. He came to my office, and said, 'Look, it's not right here.' It was the first time he had come to Francorchamps. He said, 'It's not right. It's unbelievable. In England the tracks are protected. Not like this.' And I said, 'Well, look. This is the way it is and I can't do anything about it.'

And he said, 'I'd like to get in my car and do a lap of the circuit with you and I'll tell you what's wrong.' He was in his normal clothes, not in his racing suit. It was the morning of the Friday practice session, so he was in his normal clothes. I can't remember what, exactly, but he wasn't in his driving gear. So we got in the car.

Before we got to the top it was okay because there was just forest. We were going uphill and there were pine trees. And there he said it was fine, probably because we were set back from the edge of the road. But as we got to the highest point of the track, when we started to come down, there were woods on one side and meadows on the other – with cattle, barbed wire fences . . . fence posts. There were also electricity poles.

He said, 'That's no good. If you come to England we don't have things like that. If we come off the road there's nothing in the way. It saves our lives.' And I said, 'Well, it's not like that here. People live here: there are people who live near the track.' There are houses on both sides of the track – there were then, there aren't any more – but at the time there were houses. So I said, 'There are people living here. There are farmers.'

We came back downhill to the Masta and then he said to me, 'And here: if someone comes off the track in his car, he's dead.' And I don't know if the accident with Bristow had already happened then – he came to Francorchamps. I'd have to look in my paperwork – he came to Francorchamps, I think, in 64, the first time . . .

Anyway, I don't remember if the first time he came it was before the Chris Bristow and Alan Stacey accident or if it was the following year, but I'll tell you later when I've got my papers . . . So we went on, down the hill – the home straight – and he said to me, 'Here, if someone comes off the road, he's dead. Or he'll be torn to pieces because there are fence posts, trees, etc.' And what was extraordinary – for a driver – he said to me, a bit further on, 'There's a low wall there, on the left, and then two electricity poles.' He knew by heart what was coming – better than me, and I was born here. He knew where there were posts – 'On the right there, there's another electricity pole – and then on the left there's this.' Before we even got there he knew what was coming.

Stewart said that you need to adapt the circuit to the Formula One race. There are people here that were saying that the drivers had to adapt to the track, and Stewart said it was the opposite: that the circuit had to adapt to the mechanical evolution of Formula One – and he was right.

Now I understand that it was necessary, of course, but at

the time we were so used to the track as it was. I can tell you I was born in 1922 on the circuit, and it's how I'd always known it. When Jackie Stewart said it wasn't right, it was surprising for us. We thought, 'Well, we're not in England. We're here. We've got a track and it's always worked all right since 1922.' But it didn't mean anything because everywhere – everywhere – there were changes being made. I even said, 'In Monaco, what's going on there, then?' But there, 'It's not the same.' So there you are.

At the time I didn't understand him. I thought, 'What does he want? He wants to change everything here.' Obviously – when I talked about it to the board afterwards – they said he was crazy, and I said, 'He's not as crazy as all that. He knows what he's talking about. He can see what is wrong.' And two years afterwards everyone agreed that he wasn't crazy at all. He knew exactly what he wanted. But at the time we thought that what he was talking about – what he was asking for – it wasn't possible for us. At the time.

Of course, I can understand completely why he was like that afterwards. Not only because the track was dangerous, but also because the emergency services were badly organised. That's why he had to wait twenty minutes for the ambulance to come for him. He was in his car, groggy, and they didn't come.

He wasn't happy at all about that. He was furious, understandably, because he had asked us for lots of changes before – and we hadn't done anything, or almost nothing. We hadn't taken the precautions that he wanted. There were trees that needed to be cut down. We cut down a few, but not many.

I found that what he was asking for at the time was impossible for us, because the track was managed by five different town councils: Spa, Francorchamps, Stavelot, Malmedy and another – and those towns, they didn't want to. They didn't have the money to do the work.

I thought he was asking the impossible. He asked us for things we weren't capable of doing. And I even told him that, and then he said, 'If you do nothing, we won't come back.' So I didn't say anything then, as I wasn't the Automobile Club of Belgium. I was born here. I showed him the house I was born in. I'll show it to you too, later.

He asked for all of that at the time, and I said it wasn't possible. He acknowledged that it was a long circuit and I told him that at the Nürburgring it was even longer. It's twenty-two kilometres, and here it's fourteen kilometres. And he said, 'It doesn't matter. The Nürburgring is safer than Francorchamps.' And then I said that we wouldn't be able to make any changes immediately, 'So I don't know what you're going to do.' I told him that in any case the circuit is appreciated by the drivers because it's a difficult one, and maybe they like dangerous tracks as it allows them to demonstrate their performance and their ability to drive a circuit like that.

Basically, this discussion with Stewart continued always on the same theme. He said that different circuits are necessary – testing circuits – circuits that enable drivers to assert themselves within the layout of the track. 'There are no two circuits the same. They are all different, but your track is the most dangerous of them all, even more dangerous than Nürburgring.' That's what he said to me.

Stacey and Bristow died, so we realised – nevertheless – it was dangerous. When Stewart said all that, it was already three years after the accidents involving Stacey and Bristow. So I couldn't tell him he was wrong. I tried to explain that to him, but he just kept coming back to it – Stacey and Chris Bristow. He was right: it was true. But I said that it's not because that's happened – in fact, since then there haven't been any more accidents. But he said it's just not possible. A circuit like yours is a dangerous circuit. You have to take out the walls, the trees, the fence posts . . . everything.

Then he [Stewart] came the following year and he said to me in my office, 'You know we've been round the track and you haven't done anything.' And I said, 'Yes, we have. We've cut some trees down,' and he said, 'No. You've done hardly anything,' and he was right. We didn't have the money to do everything that he wanted.

## ON THE FACILITIES AT SPA IN THE SIXTIES – TYPICAL OF THE TIME

We had a small building with just one room: a stretcher, a doctor and a surgeon. That was it. At the time there wasn't much. But some years later there was an Englishman – I forget his name – who came with a bus – a medical bus. He went to all the circuits in the world with his medical bus.

But in Stewart's time there was nothing; just a little building with a doctor. There wasn't any survival equipment . . . There was some communication. All along the circuit there were twenty-eight telephone points all linked up to each other, and also to the headquarters of the track in the tower. That wasn't where I worked. It was where those responsible for security worked. From there they would send the ambulances, or medical help – a Red Cross car.

That's how it worked. There wasn't anything else.

At the time – you have to understand – it was like on the motorways, where you had telephone posts alongside the road. It was like that. There were twenty-eight of them over fourteen kilometres, so that's one every 500 metres. And in each one there was a telephone and, next to it, a race steward. When there was an incident the telephone rang and you explained what had happened. That's why that system didn't allow us to help Jackie Stewart straight away. We sent the ambulance twenty minutes afterwards, but no one ever knew why.

## ON SPA BEING REMOVED FROM THE CHAMPIONSHIP

In 1970 – so one or two years after Jackie Stewart's accident – the Formula One Drivers' [Association], led by Jackie Stewart, decided to stop coming to Francorchamps. From 1970 to 1980, for ten years, there was no Formula One racing at Spa-Francorchamps.

Jackie Stewart wasn't alone. There were other drivers who agreed with him. They went to the FIA – the International Automobile Federation – in protest, to say that they no longer wanted to come. It wasn't just Stewart, but he was the trigger. It was sad, yes. The track continued to function, but with other sports. With prototype races . . . motorbikes.

We didn't have the money. The track is too long, and it would have been too expensive. If we had produced the kind of circuit that Stewart wanted we would have had to halve its length. It would only have been seven kilometres, which would have made it easier to protect, with fences, sandbags – everything you need.

Formula One only came back when we had reduced the circuit by half – seven kilometres instead of fourteen kilometres – and equipped the track with protective fences, sandbags etc. When it finished for those ten years, everyone protested – hotel owners, small businesses – but there was nothing to be done. We had to make a new circuit with new security measures.

## ON JACKY ICKX'S ACCIDENT

Jacky Ickx had an accident in almost the same spot as Stewart, give or take ten metres or so. But Jacky Ickx was lucky, because his car turned over, bounced, and fell on the crowd. A spectator was killed. The car was on its roof and Jacky Ickx was hanging by his seat belt. He was groggy, but not injured. That's the story of Jacky Ickx. It's pretty much the only accident he had at Francorchamps. So he never criticised Francorchamps.

I can say this about Jacky [Ickx] and Stewart. Stewart had a lot of drivers with him that thought the same as he did – that something had to be done on the track to improve protection and security. He was so demanding that drivers like Jacky Ickx and some others – Bonnier, too – they said, 'It's impossible at Francorchamps. We can't afford it.' And that's where it went wrong. Stewart had a group with him, and Ickx had a group against him.

Jacky Ickx surrounded himself with several drivers who defended the circuit – the old circuit. They defended it, while Stewart was saying, 'Something has to change. We can't carry on like this.' It was due to his presence. And Stewart won, because we changed everything. We made it all safe.

We are right in the middle of the countryside. It's a region where we work the forest. There is agriculture: there are cattle, meadows – there are farmers and lumberjacks living here and they continued to live here even during the race. So the race came through here between the houses, among the woods and the meadows.

This means that for the drivers it's extremely dangerous because if they came off the road – or if there was a collision – you could very easily end up in a field, or against a tree, or in the backyard of somebody's house. Anything was possible. For the drivers it was quite an unusual experience – especially for the British drivers, who were used to driving in completely different environments. Even American drivers like Dan Gurney were surprised to see how it was here, because they drove on oval tracks in the US. They hadn't experienced circuits like this one. There's probably only here, and Nürburgring, or that other German track – Hockenheim – that are like this. But even at Hockenheim there aren't any houses, whereas here there is everything. It's very varied.

So it was in fact a wild circuit – a track in the middle of the countryside – and when Jackie Stewart saw it for the first time he said, 'It's dangerous here because it's not safeguarded. There are houses, trees, electricity pylons. For me it's a very dangerous track.' That's what Stewart said to me. We cut the trees that were right next to the track. All along this road here there were apple trees, and the people who lived here harvested the apples – and when we wanted to cut the apple trees down they didn't agree, so it was a bit of a war. And finally we got the agreement and we cut them down.

I was born in 1922, the year of the very first race on the circuit – the first car race. I told him all of that, but he wasn't interested. What he wanted . . . no more fence posts, no more trees, no more houses or nothing. Either that, or we had to change everything. It was impossible at the time, and I told him so.

It was the end of something, yes. It's true that for years we thought that it would remain unchanged. All circuits have their own characteristics, so the drivers of the time had never really criticised the differences between them. But there were serious accidents that occurred here, as was the case with Stacey and Chris Bristow. Before those accidents there had never been any deaths on this circuit in Formula One. Formula One began in 1950 and Stacey and Bristow are the first two Formula One drivers who got killed here. So for Jackie Stewart it was important. He was saying that if it had happened to those two then there would be others because it's seriously dangerous at your track.

# 5

# JOHN SURTEES OBE

*John Surtees was an important interviewee as he did not necessarily share all of Jackie Stewart's views on safety, and he talks openly about Jackie not being the only driving force for safety. John has a different viewpoint, as he was not only a world champion driver and motorcyclist but has been a manufacturer. John was involved with Honda and the tragic death of Jo Schlesser, and his own son died in a racing accident in 2009. He also describes the relationship a racer can have with a machine.*

## ON THE SIXTIES

The Triumph Herald was being built at that time, and so Triumph steering racks and uprights became a standard component in Formula One. You could never imagine that – but you have to remember that you had the complete change, where you had manufacturers building cars where they would come along and actually machine a set of wishbones. So you had the Maserati and the Mercedes and the Ferraris all coming along and building very well-engineered cars, but basically the cars of the fifties were all 1930s technology – an extension of what had happened at the beginning of the war. Those cars were quite fantastic.

The first words that Ferrari said to me when I first went

there – and they asked me for a second time, as I had turned them down first time – 'You see our factory? It will all be behind you, but we don't have a lot of money.' So you're talking an age when you win a world championship, and you perhaps won £25,000 – a lot of money then. But just the same, quite different from what the scene is today.

When I won my first Grand Prix in the Ferrari, after three laps my overalls were soaked in petrol. The tank over my knees had cracked due to the state of the circuit. This was the sort of thing that happened at that time, so we have to be thankful that there has been a lot of development and research and money gone into [it].

People in our time would be thinking about racing their Formula One car and they would be thinking about driving F2 cars or another type of car. We used to drive all sorts of cars. When I joined Ferrari I was out testing the prototype cars for Le Mans. Or at the Nürburgring I would be testing an F1 car and then a road car would come up and I would go off and test that. We kept a busy life, although there were less Grands Prix. We raced in other categories, so it was a different way of life. The way it is today an F1 driver is an F1 driver, full stop.

## ON JIM CLARK

We became great friends. When I first married, Jim was my best man at my wedding, and I said that was the only time I would admit to him being best man. Jim loved his motor racing and the driving part of it. He didn't like the business and political side of it, but he was a good lad on and off the track. I didn't stay so close to him when I joined Ferrari but, with hindsight, maybe I should have stayed put in 1960 when I had the opportunity.

## ON SPEED

When it comes down to motor sport – whether it be two, three or four wheels – you are in partnership with the machine and you have to understand each other. Some machines have characters where you place trust in them. Others have characters where you are constantly striving to get to one hundred per cent trust. But basically you can't be too sure of them or the way you have to develop your car, and you have to change your style of driving to suit the various characteristics that come up. So to me the biggest satisfaction – and it all started with bikes – is that relationship with the machinery. It has to be one which virtually talks to you: 'I'm on the limit here. Don't push it any more.' And you do get that . . . where it's just the pair of you – you and the machine – that's the most satisfying thing.

Spa is a prime circuit for that, when you get a car or a bike that is set up . . . The bike would start moving and you would start to drift at 160 mph – and if you look at photos you have just a bit of opposite lock, because the bike's going through the corner just slightly drifting. Same thing with a car – and you can get it on the limit and you have to read it by the seat of the pants and the feeling that it gives to you. That is one of the nicest partnerships, when a machine is really responding to you. Spa, particularly with the high speed corners, was one that was very satisfying.

Yeah, I love Spa. I have won there on motorcycles and cars. I drove sports cars and F1 cars there. You had to be careful as it could be dry on a corner but wet on the next. The challenge of Spa was very special. To get it right was very satisfying when you had the car or the bike just on the limit. So yes, Spa was special – and not far from it, the Nürburgring was also very special.

In those days you didn't have wet and dry tyres. You had one pattern of tyre, though you had different makes: Dunlop and Firestones, but mainly it was Dunlop. One tyre when it really rained – it could be really difficult. We had a dry start at the 66 Grand Prix [at Spa] and I took the lead – and then going up the hill after the start you go up to the top of the hill, turn right, and go back down into the valley.

In those days you turned left and dropped down into a very long fast corner called Bourneville, and approaching that the spits of rain came on to my goggles. The obvious thing then was to make certain you didn't put too much lock, and you would try and get off the racing line because the roads would be a bit more grippy. So I went through there and down the main straight – and it was down the back straight and through the village where a number of incidents took place, including the one with Jackie Stewart.

But I never saw any of that as I was up front with Jochen Rindt, who was in the Cooper Maserati behind me. It then intensified in rain and I actually deliberately backed off and Jochen – in the spirit of youth – went steaming by, and I just sat in his wheel tracks for a few laps while the heaviest of the rain went off. I then sped up and had a good win, but it was to be my last race for Ferrari as after that I had a massive disagreement with the management.

I didn't see any of the accidents – but yes, people ended up in ditches and things like that. If you get caught out in a certain rainstorm it can happen. It wasn't a vast number: it was two or three people who had spins. I suppose Jackie was extremely vocal about what had happened as it had been a frightening experience for him. At that stage the cars of the sixties were not that safe. They were, I suppose, state of the art for that time – very much kit cars that had been put together without much thought for the safety.

## ON JACKIE STEWART'S STRIVING FOR SAFETY

Some good things came out of it. Some bad things. Good things were the attention to the medical side and the speed of it, and you have to blame the governing body for not being as stringent as they should have been . . . but the Spa circuit was a very experienced one, but fell down on not getting things done quick enough.

I went to circuits around the world and you would have photographers – even spectators – that were so close that if you took certain lines you had to move your body to make sure you didn't catch a camera or somebody else as you went by. There were no safety features. My first race in 1950 at the new Brands Hatch – there's pictures of me sitting on the start line, and there's fencing running along the side of the track for the spectators to stand behind.

Things [like] petrol pouring out: that could have happened in any car – and luckily for Jackie it didn't catch fire, because in the sixties you did have a lot of fires. All this drastically changed when you got to the end of the seventies. A whole new generation of cars came about and you had safety measures coming in – in the seventies and eighties – which is like you see today.

Jackie had his own little group of support, and this largely dictated some of the things that happened. But at least he was following his own convictions. The fact that I thought different is another thing, but it could have done with others having some input – standing up and being counted – but it didn't happen.

Jackie had his agenda. Jackie was a competent driver, and I didn't agree with him on a number of his views. I thought his ideas about guard rails were wrong and that was basically that. At least Jackie voiced an opinion. The problem with the GPDA was that people would go to a meeting and not say a dicky bird and then afterwards complain. The GPDA could have done with more input, and one of the reasons that Jackie got away with excesses was because others were willing to not take the whole thing seriously.

The bad thing that came out of Spa was lining everywhere with guard rails. That was horrific. I thought, 'Yes . . . guard rails used in the right place is fine, but looking at them as the answer to problems?' I mean, if Jackie had guard rails where he went off [at Spa] he would probably have had a far bigger accident and the petrol would have caught fire. But the fact remains: for motorcyclists they were horrific, and they were used indiscriminately instead of in places where, together with other measures, they provided an added safety factor – which was my opinion, and one I expressed at the time.

When you go along and a lot of the resources aren't there, there is very little you can do about it. The people who called the tune were the people who ran the race at Nürburgring or at Spa. They were largely all-powerful. Lots of changes had come about. It's not perfect today. I have unfortunately been involved in an accident with my son where – again, on safety issues – there are things you can question, but not to the degree that existed in the sixties.

But it's progress. Just look what happens today in F1 and you see what people can escape from. That largely came about through money. Money was created in F1 where it never previously existed. People were largely running teams hand to mouth. The engineers got together: new technology was brought into it . . . and we had the safety cell. Tremendous advantages, but it would not have happened if it was not for the worldwide appeal through TV and the money.

## ON THE GRAND PRIX DRIVERS' ASSOCIATION

The GPDA meetings were a group which should have been quite serious. Generally, it wasn't. You often found people falling asleep, and when it came to a vote they would wake up and put their hand up. So you didn't get the seriousness that the subject deserved. I don't think it had a very big influence. Things did develop relative to the support. Some of the early attempts to make sure you had proper medical attendants – to make sure you had everything available at the circuit – these things were all in motion and happening. To start with there was a mobile unit which used to travel around to all the circuits – because the races did not extend to rushing off to China and Japan, etc. in those days. So improvements did take place and detailed improvements on circuits took place, but not inspired by one single force. I think the guard rail side was largely inspired by Jackie Stewart, but this was a common objective with all the drivers.

The fact that Grand Prix drivers have an association is a good thing, just like the constructors have an association. It was important to have somewhere where you exchanged ideas. I always thought, because I have been a member of both, that neither the drivers really achieved what could have been achieved – and the constructors' side went on from that, of course. Constructors becoming united . . . led to probably the biggest safety advances that took place.

A driver is contracted to a team – so they should in fact be working with the teams, as they should have a common interest. So it's right the drivers have a periodical meeting and discuss points that come up and recommend them through. But as such they are not in a position to come along and take a militant attitude and do too much in regard to regulations.

I was representing foreign companies, as I wasn't part of the British group – where the majority of teams were all based. The only time I was only competing for a British team was in 1960-62. From 63 – when you talk about Grand Prix Drivers' Association things – I was with a foreign team and I was a bit of the odd man out. You had people who were travelling en bloc and interchanging ideas more, and the British team were closer together than those who were involved in a foreign team. So the GPDA . . . some interesting things were discussed. I don't think it achieved an awful lot but it was still something that was important because the original structure was not good.

It was a big deal [when Nürburgring was removed from Grand Prix] because the Nürburgring was a very special place that attracted an enormous crowd of people, and it was something that was important. It's wrong to suggest that in motor sport you had a lot of militancy. You have had movements for change but largely the change all came about once you started getting into the late seventies, and to see changes that came about by the Constructors' Association. The way that organisation and the way motor sport was marketed . . . it was put on to a bigger business footing than it was before. Before there was separate entities who were played against each other . . . the people that brought change about were the constructors, not the drivers' association.

## ON SPA BEING REMOVED FROM GRAND PRIX

I think it was a sad day for motorsport. I think in motorsport you have to think that the past and the present are merged in a way that we do not lose too much. In F1 you need to have as natural a circuit as can be with some safety features put in – with a bit of history. To see a race at Spa even on camera – it's something special, and you mustn't lose Spa or Le Mans. Luckily, Spa – although the old circuit didn't survive . . . the new circuit is a very good modern circuit. It has some of the features of the old one and has been made usable [for] this day and age.

It was a big deal when it got removed, but commercial forces made it difficult for these circuits to compete. In Spa in 1960 I was racing in a motorcycle race, so I didn't go – and my car was driven by Stacey, who got killed in that race. You have to remember 1960-1966 – when the accident with Jackie happened – we are talking six years. In that time Jackie had been to Spa before. You had these accidents, but it was considered mechanical – or perhaps a bird had hit a driver. They were not particularly pointing the finger at Spa. In 1966 a few got into trouble in the rain – it happens in most wet races. A lot didn't. A lot came through okay.

Certainly the delay in getting attention to the accident that involved Jackie was to be deplored.

## ON LOTUS AND CHAPMAN

Colin Chapman came along and said, 'Try an F1 car.' So I turned up at Silverstone and Colin was there and I went out and did some laps. And Colin did some laps and Colin said, 'You're my driver.' I said, 'I'm not, really. I'm riding motorcycles. I'm in the world championships and the TT.' So he said, 'You are my driver when you are not racing motorcycles.' So we shook hands and I became a Lotus driver. We went to Silverstone and the oil pump failed, so that wasn't very good.

At Lotus we were involved in a lot of mechanical failures. But when a Lotus 18 was going as it should it was a wonderful car, and probably the most competitive car in the field. Certainly for a new boy to come along and be able to lead Grands Prix and finish second . . . it not only reflected on me, but on the car. The Lotus 18 was fragile but still a very fine motor car, and that fragility image stayed with Lotus for a while. It largely disappeared, as Lotus developed a lot. Colin was a very infectious character. I regretted I didn't stay because he showed so much enthusiasm and drive. It was rather special, that first year – 1960.

## ON HONDA

It was a different era. Cooper and Lotus – which were the two British teams that came up – they were the new boys.

They were garden shed-type constructors to start with, but they developed. I invested part of my life in Honda and left Ferrari. I expected to stay at Ferrari for the rest of my life but this political situation arose. Afterwards I made it up with the old man and he said we must remember the good times and not the bad, as my leaving Ferrari cost him two world championships and me the same – because we had that chance of a couple or more championships together.

I went to Honda and became partly responsible for organising the team and doing all the general team liaison with Tokyo and the development programme, and it was very good at times. But also frustrating, as Tokyo is a long way away – and to get the message over was very difficult. We had a good team in this country, but just the same we struggled with the sense of urgency of getting everything going in Japan.

We started off with a very heavy car. Today people talk about cars having five litres more of petrol in them, and it affects the performance. We had something like 170 lbs overweight, so you are talking a substantial sum. For 68 we produced another car, which is one of the sad things in my life in a way . . . in that car, apart from some of the stupid problems we had, it could have taken us to a potential challenge for the championship.

It was still overweight – but we had lots of silly problems, which were partly human. Honda used motorsport very much to train people as much as for the publicity, so we had lots of new people coming through – and people, when they are learning, make mistakes – so this lost us some races. In the end it stood Honda very well, as we had a lot of trained people. We were then coming up to the point where I thought we would have the ultimate car, which was a development of the last two years and would be down to weight. And then a political thing at Honda changed all this. A car was made which wasn't suitable for racing – and after I said it wasn't suitable to run they gave it to someone else, and that person was killed in it. That was Schlesser, and that happened in the French Grand Prix.

How the accident happened was . . . the French took over the car and they ran it for their French driver. There was an unfortunate accident which killed him, but on top of that tragedy it meant that the Honda race programme just stopped. So all the investment and time came to nothing. That was when I started to think about building our own F1 car.

There was a conflict between the engineers. One lot said one thing: the other set of engineers, who were associated with me, said something else. It was a concept car, which had some interesting features on it and could have been quite useful to use as a research car, but it was not suitable for racing.

It was an air-cooled car, which was to be air- and oil-cooled. It didn't work – and the engine, although it produced good power for one lap . . . it would then fail because of major problems in the cooling side.

It wasn't the original design: it was a design made to fit in with a commercial objective, because a road car was going to be developed like that. But it was not a concept that was created by the race team – it was developed by the commercial team.

I wasn't very pleased at the time. No, I wasn't pleased. Because – if you channel all your effort into one thing – you should be doing it as a team. But it happens in life, where people pull in opposite directions, and that was sad.

I maintained good relationships with Honda. I admire what Mr Honda did in creating Honda, the same as how Mr Ferrari created Ferrari. But they didn't always get the answers right, and in that case Mr Honda didn't get the answer right.

# 6

# JEAN-PIERRE BELTOISE

*Jean-Pierre had a similar sentiment to Jackie Stewart when it came to safety matters. His candid interview is translated from the original French.*

In my racing, from the 1960s until 1973, there were many deaths. It's the accumulative effect that makes you aware gradually that you could die, even if it's not your fault – a car breaks, oil on the track . . . something like that. So it just added to the danger of it all, and the fact that one day you could die.

A driver is often confronted by death. And on top of that I had already lost my first wife a few years before . . . my brother, who was just next to me in age – I had four brothers – when I was twenty-five years old. So death had already affected me greatly. Plus other drivers who were friends – like Jo Schlesser, who I liked a lot. Lots of young French drivers . . . all these young drivers. So I was already very hardened to death. Jim Clark was the most important. Personally we liked him a lot, but it just added to it all.

I had already had to face death for several years by then, so you stop experiencing it as something new that you don't expect. It became something we expected around us, unfortunately. Most of all my first wife: when she died, she was very young. I had just started racing and I remember I raced in Pau in Formula Two eight days afterwards. It was very difficult. Unfortunately, at that time we were prepared for it and I think it's perhaps the greatest difference between drivers of that era and nowadays. Now you hardly think any more about getting killed at the wheel.

When I look at photos taken in my era – out of twenty drivers, ten of them are dead. Half of them. It's awful. You don't see things in the same way. We were completely prepared for death without even thinking about it. Or if we did think that we could get killed on a dangerous track – not Zandvoort, like you mentioned – but the Nürburgring, or Clermont-Ferrand or Rouen-Les-Essarts, it occurred to us – but the thought goes straight out of your head. We slept very well the night before. No problem. But we knew that maybe on the Sunday evening we would be gone, so you would think about it a little bit – about your wife and children being all alone, and how awful it would be.

When I receive photos from fans . . . photos from 68, 69, 70 – and I see the spectators right at the edge of the track, and it's unbelievable. It seems like it must be a fake photo, it is so unbelievable . . . absolutely unthinkable nowadays. So things changed very quickly, and the drivers that we were – with the Grand Prix Drivers' Association meetings and Jackie Stewart, who was very active when I was with him . . . to get things to change quickly, because the safety conditions were just impossi- ble. And the managers at the time didn't intend to improve them. They weren't in the cars. I always used to say, 'In order for the track managers to understand how dangerous it is we need to take them in the cars at real speed. Only then will they do something.'

## ON JIM CLARK

I was there and at the time we were very close, because my wife and I had just got married. And Jimmy really wanted us to get married, and every time we were together he would say little things about it. [When he was killed] It was quite a painful moment because we really liked him – and we were close because of all the Formula Two races, so we would see each other a lot. First of all, no one expected it. It was on a straight, so we don't really know what happened. He went off into the forest and it was against a tree, I think. There weren't the safety measures that there should have been, but we don't know why he came off the track at that particular spot. It was bad luck, and maybe a part on the car was broken. I don't know. I don't remember. But it was a very difficult time because Jimmy was a demigod. He was the best driver among us at the time. For us he was like Juan Manuel Fangio. Like a god. It was impossible for him to get killed. It was hard . . . unbelievable.

Jim Clark got killed during the practice . . . I can't remember any more about it because I was so taken up with the race . . . when I was at the start I didn't think of it when racing. I put it out of my mind. You're just in the car with one idea in your head: to win the race. You're concentrating on the present. The difficulty, which is that of the racing driver, is to drive as best you can so that you win. It's only at the finish that you think about it. Once it's all over you think about it then.

On top of that I think that the next day – I'm sure of it now – I won the race. It was a Formula Two race. It's only afterwards you think about it. But you know drivers are like that: they are concentrating so much they even forget about

illness. You chase away germs. I often raced when I was ill –
when I had flu – but when I was driving I drove it away. I felt
ill beforehand, taking aspirin and everything – and at the end
of the race I thought I was better . . . cured. I always thought
that, and then one – two – hours later, the germs came back
and I had flu again. It's the same about horrible thoughts. If
you lose someone very dear to you, like I did with my first
wife or with Jimmy Clark, you put it from your mind when
you're at the start line. You absolutely do not think about
it: you are just thinking of being focused, concentrated,
determined to win the race.

## ON GOING FAST

The goal is to go as fast as possible. So speed doesn't count.
It's being the fastest. In my case I started riding my bike with
the neighbours, my friends and my brothers in the garden.
The speed is very slow, twenty kilometres per hour at the
most, on gravel. You go faster and faster, but you never see
the speed. Even when you're at much greater speeds, like 300
kilometres per hour or more, you are so used to it that you
don't see the track go by – you don't see the people around the
track. You just see the track – the car that you are controlling
– and you don't realise the speed. You only realise the speed
when you have a suspension problem or there is oil on the
track and you lose control – and then, suddenly, the speed
is terrifying, because you are not in control any more. And
then you say to yourself – and it's happened to me several
times – 'I'm going to get hurt. What a speed. I'm going to get
hurt.'

But as long as you are driving, even at 300 kilometres per

hour . . . I'm sure that even at Indianapolis, where they go at 400 kilometres per hour, the drivers don't feel like they are going at great speed. The sensation of speed comes gradually. For example, when you start to drive, if you are used to eighty kilometres per hour it is very difficult to imagine going at 120 kilometres per hour. Fifty per cent faster seems impossible – you don't look ahead enough. You don't anticipate enough. You don't have enough time to react with the pedals. Then, going from 120 kilometres per hour to 160 kilometres per hour – to 250 kilometres per hour to 350 kilometres per hour . . . each time the problem is there. But it's not a problem: it's a habit that you pick up very quickly.

I have a very Cartesian mind: realistic. For me things are anchored, without uncertainty. When you can't see in front of you there is a lot of uncertainty. I've been very affected by that, which is why I don't like the Le Mans 24 Hours, because driving at night there is a lot of uncertainty. You can't see the road, or if there is oil on it you can't see that. My first Le Mans, which I won in a small car, I saw a Brazilian in front of me get killed on a hairpin off the straight because he didn't see oil on the road. He didn't see it, but when I came up behind – 500 metres behind him – I saw the yellow flags everywhere. You can't see oil at night. I saw that I could get by so I didn't take my foot off – and I went past at full speed and all of a sudden I lost control of the car, like he did. And, ever since, I've always hated the uncertainty of driving in the rain or at night. It's too dangerous, especially in my era. Now the cars are stronger. The crash barriers keep the cars on the track. Maybe it's more acceptable, but still difficult to accept.

Juan Manuel Fangio or someone said that if you are a courageous driver you'll get killed right away. You don't need to be courageous. You need to be realistic about the problems, not brave. When a driver is in his car – if he's decided to make a career out of the sport – he's there to win. When he's in the car at the start line, he's not thinking at all about what could happen to him. He's only thinking of doing the best he possibly can: to be as close as possible to the guys in front and to be the first, if possible. There is no notion of courage in a driver's mind. Never. Just a question of technical precision – of driving with precision, which means that when you are coming up to a big bend – at Spa-Francorchamps, for example – which was a terrific circuit, where all the bends were pretty much at full speed – it's not bravery going at full speed. It's technical precision. It's true that there might be a little desire not to take your foot off at a big corner – not to brake – but honestly, for me, it's not courage. It's the desire to do better than the previous lap. That's it.

The nerves before a race, feeling a bit sick inside – it's because you want to do the best you possibly can. That's nothing to do with danger. The danger is dealt with beforehand. Your body is emptied of everything else – like an artist about to go on stage, with the aim of succeeding in what you are about to do. And for every driver – as for every artist – this difficult feeling disappears as soon as you begin – a minute before the start, or as soon as you come out on stage.

## ON JO SCHLESSER

When Jo Schlesser got killed at Rouen-Les-Essarts he was killed on the second or third lap, with the Honda that was made completely of magnesium. He burnt in the car. And for the whole race we could smell burning flesh. Each time we arrived at the bends it was horrible. I don't know why, but I thought it might be Jo Schlesser. I don't know what was wrong. The car wasn't good: I wasn't in a good position to win the race, nor be in the first three or four. I just wanted it to be over. I was afraid it was Jo who was dead. I stopped at the stands. It's the only time in my life I ever did that, with no other reason than to ask, 'Who got killed? Is it Jo?' And they said, 'No, it's not Jo.' So I carried on, half reassured. I had been reassured, but not enough. I wanted to know. And of course it was Jo who had died. I found out at the end. They did well to tell me that it wasn't him. He was a good friend.

## ON JACKIE STEWART CLOSING DOWN CIRCUITS

Among the drivers who are still alive, that are around me, I have a very good relationship with Jackie Stewart – but the two I am most friendly with are Henri Pescarolo and Jacky Ickx, maybe because we speak the same language and we see each other more frequently. But Henri Pescarolo and Jacky Ickx have different feelings to mine – which are more like the feelings of Jackie Stewart – or like Mark Webber today, who are drivers who are more realistic about the problems. Henri Pescarolo and Jacky Ickx are more like, 'As God wills it.'

'That's life, as God wills it.' . . . They weren't vigilant about safety – at least, that's the impression that I have. Stewart and I were very vigilant about safety, and today I am very proud of what we did for track safety.

Jackie Stewart had a great aura. He was world champion: he was well-respected. So what he said carried a lot of weight. He was right to do it. I was less important but I also went quite far, at the Fédération Internationale pour le Sport d'Automobile, to accredit the circuits – and I remember I was in discussion with those technically and politically responsible and I was very tough with them. I remember, and I'm not afraid to say it, that I was responsible for closing down Clermont-Ferrand. After eight hours of discussion . . . there was one gentleman on the committee called Herbert, I think – I think he was German – who I got on well with – but I couldn't make myself heard around the table to say that if they wanted to continue at Clermont-Ferrand they had to do this and that.

They said it was too expensive and I said it had to be done. At one point we both ended up going to the toilets, and I was saying – as we were stood at the urinals . . . I said to him, 'You can't continue with the views that you have. Imagine that your son becomes a Formula One driver, and he gets killed, and you know it's your fault. You can't argue with that.' When he went back he said, 'Beltoise is right. We have to make these changes.' And Clermont-Ferrand was cancelled. But we couldn't always talk in that way around the table. I'm sure Jackie Stewart was always very firm and he was right to be. I think he would have approved of my actions.

## ON AERODYNAMICS

The major difference, around 69 or so, was when the engineers Chapman and Jim Hall understood the importance of aerodynamics. That was the seminal moment. When they started to put wings on – rework the body of the cars so they were closer to the ground – 1970 was a turning point for that era. Before that the cars were round, beautiful, relying on mechanical grip for traction. And then with aerodynamics everything changed, everything developed – and it was an important moment in automobile racing.

Before, in the 1960s – when John Cooper raced the first cars with the engine in the middle – while Ferrari, BRM still had engines at the front . . . that was to have more power by having the weight of the motor above the rear wheels. That wasn't a revolution. That was a normal evolution, but downforce – or aerodynamics: we thought of dynamics as penetrating the air . . . we didn't think of it as pushing the car down towards the ground.

That was in 1970, and it was the extreme revolution in automobile racing. I'd say it was a shame in terms of spectacle – maybe also in terms of safety, because the cars went so quickly into the bends that you had to make enormous spaces around the track so that the cars didn't impact so hard outside the track. But that was the revolution. It was amazing. Downforce.

In the seventies they started to think about bringing the cars closer to the ground, but they hadn't understood they could do that with the bodywork of the car. So they added wings, sometimes very high on the car. I remember Graham Hill's accident in Barcelona – one of the last accidents to kill people in the crowd, because he went right over the crash barriers. But under the influence of Jim Hall and Colin Chapman the constructors quickly understood that the cars should be brought closer to the ground.

Between the trials and the race you could take things off the car – for example, if it was slowing the car down, or if the car was not well balanced. I never took the decision to take things off like Rindt did, but I knew my car without the wings was not very good. In 69 you could still do it. By 1970 it wasn't possible.

## ON CRASH BARRIERS

When François Cevert – my brother-in-law – was killed, it was because the barriers were of very low quality. They were not rigid enough; they were too flexible. They also have to be set up in such a way that guides the car. They shouldn't bend or sway, or lift up. At Jarama I stopped. Jackie Stewart had just gone off the track. He must remember that day, because he was incredibly lucky. He went right into it. The car was right under the barrier and the barrier was in front of his face. He was within twenty centimetres of being crushed, in spite of his helmet between the crash barrier and his headrest. So there were all these sorts of problems. Sure, there were a lot of deaths. Jochen Rindt, François Cevert – and others still, that have miraculously escaped.

My last race, at Watkins Glen – one year after François's death – I came out of the BRM car, off the track – I don't know how – and under the safety barrier, like Jackie Stewart. I was stuck. Luckily, the car didn't burn. Otherwise, I would have been dead. They had to pull the shell off the car and to get my shoes off so that I could get out. At the time it was like that. Nowadays there is much more care paid – not only to the big safety principles but also on the long straights, where walls or crash barriers are there to guide the cars.

## ON SEAT BELTS AND FIRE

I honestly don't remember if we had seat belts or not. I can't remember the first time we used them. Didn't we have them at Hockenheim? Incredible. In 68? It was around that time they came in. I had an accident in Reims where the car was totally destroyed. I didn't have a seat belt and I was ejected from a closed car. I don't know how. I'm not dead and it's true that it's better to have seat belts, but maybe if I had had one that day at Reims then I might have burnt in the car.

They are absolutely necessary, of course. No need for discussion on how effective they are: in safety terms, the greatest progress. We knew that if we crashed we could burn. When I was in the BRM I was always afraid the car would catch fire. Always. There were so many. The young English driver Williamson, at Zandvoort. It was horrible. Jo Schlesser, too. Fire was dreadful.

When a car crashed hard enough, most of the time it went up in flames. It was just like that. So the Federation and the constructors thought it through – to make soft tanks that didn't explode, flexible connections, etc. It's amazing today that when you think about it – the impact in modern races – that the cars don't explode.

## ON QUITTING GRAND PRIX

We loved the sport, but too many have been killed. Perhaps the last accident was Ayrton Senna, but in my time it was Bruce McLaren, Jim Clark, Jochen Rindt. That's what pushed us to do something. That's a reaction you can have, when it's too dangerous. I stopped F1 when Matra decided to stop racing. It was January fifteenth, right at the beginning of the season – and all the good teams already had drivers signed up. I could only sign up for less good ones at the bottom of the table. And I thought it was too dangerous, so I stopped because of that. It would have been stupid.

I'd managed to stay alive, whereas really great drivers and

friends like Jim Clark and Jochen Rindt were dead – so I thought I'd better not play with fire. So I stopped F1 because of that. If I could have got into the top three cars to try to become world champion I would have, but to continue racing just to be in Formula One – but not with a car that enabled me to win races – that didn't interest me. I stopped at the end of 74 or 75.

We were motivated by the idea that we could make it to become the best driver in the world. Of course, it was nice to be around pretty girls or go to places where we got a good reception – because at the time we were invited to the governors' palaces – places like that – which was very pleasant. But I wasn't really into that. The only really important thing for me was how I could win races.

The first time I met my wife it was not far from here, in a motorbike shop – where François Cevert, her brother, used to go to look at bikes. Jacqueline was very pretty when she was younger – and I remember seeing this young girl in the shop, but I only noticed her for about three or four seconds because I had come to choose a bike. I had a race coming up and I had come to prepare my bike for the race. That's what I was there for. So it was a nice little spark.

The luck I had was to be totally in love with my driving. I was determined to be the best and it changed my life, compared to what it could have been. All the more so as I'm still alive, which is fantastic. When you're still alive, life is good.

There are many memories, but it's only now I start to look at the photos.

# 7
# JACKY ICKX

Jacky Ickx

*This was not an easy interview for either me or Jacky. We had been to Paris where we had met Jacqueline Beltoise, who was telling us about all the sadness and loss. I think Jacky thought I was being negative. However, a lot of our interviewees had a lot to say on the subject of danger and loss and were very open about it.*

I am a great admirer of Jimmy [Clark] still today. I have plenty of thoughts about him. Real gentleman. Charming. The best in that era. Seeing people like that having those sorts of accidents was just not acceptable. That's the reason why things changed.

That's a very good question: to see how in forty-five years things have changed. We were supposed to be professionals at the time. The cars were supposed to be at the top. When you look backwards to F2 or F3, I think today it will be ten times more professional than the F1 or the long-distance GT40 [of those times]. We were pure amateurs. We were called professionals, but we were total amateurs.

For me, I don't speak about it [the past]. It is forgotten, and I don't spend my time thinking about how it was. It was part of my life, but I am not that person any more. I am not the Jacky Ickx of yesterday. If I was going to reach the age of sixty-five and still think about an era of fifty years ago . . . I think it's finished. Behind us. Let's go to the future.

It's pointless to live in the past. To live in the present and future is the interesting thing in life. I am not convinced I think you can learn on your own good experiences. I don't think you can live in motor racing on things that have happened in the past. All the stories from the sixties are behind us.

I was able to change [from racing] and I went to the Paris-Dakar, for example. Much more interesting. I needed to discover that there were other things in life. I have 180 degree vision of the world, and I am happy. I am opening myself to another world. Because if you stay only concentrated on what you do well in motor racing what does it represent? It's a microworld. It's important to see the world differently.

Clearly the way to success first is to be in the right team and the right car. Between being a participant and being one of the few good drivers who can reach the victory is another subject. To me the aim of sport is to be on the podium. I will add to that that sometimes people ask questions about the speed, which you get used to quickly. The real goal in this or any sport is to win, even in normal life.

As far as I am concerned I came to racing in a very unexpected way. I wasn't dreaming about being a race driver. I was not successful at school but I discovered success through motorcycling. When I was sixteen I started to compete in motorcycle races and I became quickly world rider for Zündapp and Grand Prix also. I was one of the great admirers of Sammy Miller and Gordon Jackson. Then someone came with the offer to drive a car and I did it reasonably successfully. Then I went through the different categories of motor racing and then – honestly – I think the man who really changed my career was Ken Tyrrell. He offered me a test that I couldn't do because I was going into the army. A year later I came back and tried a Cooper at Goodwood in 1965, in winter.

I always had a good time because I am one of these lucky guys who always had a good time – because I was always in the right cars. What you have to understand that at the time there was no exclusivity, no team driving and no sponsors. We were free to go where we wanted, so it's probably nice to say I started going long-distance in Ford GT40s, Ford Mirage, Formula Two with Ken [Tyrrell], and Maserati, Brabham . . . five years with Ferrari, so it's hard to say you are not a lucky guy.

In summary of all that the goal is not only to race with good cars, but also to survive in that year.

## ON JACKIE STEWART

When we meet Jackie Stewart or other people from the era, the first thing we can say is that we can burn a candle every day – because to survive, it's not a question of talent. It's a question of pure luck. My friends at the time – at that era – if we survived, we were extremely lucky.

It was totally unacceptable. In the fifties or sixties it was accepted to lose two or three drivers every year. I cannot understand why we are arguing about that today.

The basic idea is to stay alive. I wouldn't say that there was one hundred per cent support from everyone. He was the president of the GPDA at the time and he had everyone hassling about it. Basically, I think he was right. We had some conflicts at the time, and conflicts of making moves forward, but on the principle . . . yes. We can say today two men who were the key in motorsport: one is Jackie Stewart and two is Jean-Marie Balestre, who was the president of the Automobile Federation at the time. These two really made moves and the reason why racing is so safe today is because originally two people wanted to succeed, and they did.

He [Stewart] was intelligent and clearly he wanted to survive – and he did what he felt was right at the time, and probably it was not approved of. He was extremely brave. He did what he needed to do: he upset a lot of people because they had to move their arses to get it done. Really, he did an outstanding job.

## ON SPA WHEN JACKIE STEWART CRASHED

Yes, it was tough – because sometimes it's raining on one side of the course and dry on the other side, and without any warning all these cars in the 1967 [66] were going flat out . . . it was raining and almost everyone crashed and it was just pure luck that nobody died that day because there had been no information about the rain at the time. Without major improvement the drivers did not want to go back to Spa unless they were going to work on it – so they did.

## ON CHAPMAN AND LOTUS

He isn't there any more to talk about it. He would have been the right person to talk about it. I won't discuss, but we know that there were extremely good cars – but also they were so fragile that it wasn't really funny to drive the cars. On the track there were a number of mechanical failures that were unacceptable.

I drove for Lotus from 74 to 75 and I had a number of mechanical failures at the time, and it's a little bit embarrassing. It's not a question of being . . . of being faulty.

When you are sharing the same spirit with the team you share the motivation of the mechanic and the engineer and you want to have the best possible score – but you have to feel safe and comfortable in the car, and that aspect was not really easy.

It's a clear opinion of what was Colin Chapman, because he was a genius in a way and he had plenty of ideas. He never stopped and that's the reason why he won so many races with drivers. He is a genius.


## ON SUCCESS AND SURVIVING

You don't build up a big friendship with people in motorsport at that time. You do things together but you don't really get the friendship because you never know what is going to happen next month. Is your driver going to be there or not be there? So, for people who have a minimum of sentimentality, you don't try to build up a too-close relationship.

That's the reason why you cannot choose. Things happen. You feel like you build up your own destiny, but basically that's not true. The people surrounding you are the best: you have the possibility to say 'Yes' or 'No.' You have to be there at the right time and you cannot force things, so you have some options. The timing – your speed on the track – is the most important thing. If people believe you can win, then – okay – you have some offers. You can choose sometimes between one or two makes of car and then – okay – you can say 'Yes' or not, but you cannot dream of Ferrari and then to drive for them. These sorts of things happen and then you pick up what is the correct choice.

The point I was making was just to say that I consider it a privilege of any kind of motor sport, cycle or single-seater or whatever . . . *with* my teammates we won more than fifty races. With my teammates. You have to be in the right place for these decisions. You are there because someone thinks you are the right person, and very often I was that. More than that is to be able to say, 'Yes, I have done the sixties, seventies, eighties era and am here to tell you how it was.' It is a pure privilege. By luck. Only by luck.

All the people who are here today will have the same answer. It's not a matter of talent. The talent will not stop you from having an accident or having a mechanical failure here or there. That's what we all say. It's just a privilege.

At the time, for sure, if you had any kind of fear or instinct of survival you have to choose another sport. I truly believe that at that level, especially motor sport, you have to be young – and you shouldn't have any fear. You should have plenty of dreams.

I have to remind you because I don't think you have listened. In this era these talented drivers were dying every year and it was part of it, but still not acceptable.

When you are young you have dreams. The sport is made for young people. You have limited instinct of preservation. You have your dreams and you are ready for it. Don't confuse things. We didn't do it because it was dangerous. We weren't thinking about it. We knew it. Nobody forced us to do it. You do it because you are good at it.

From the start of this conversation we are only talking about the danger. There are other things and danger is only part of it. If this interview is only to be about danger and risk and so on we can stop. You keep going back. It's very upsetting. There are many more pleasant aspects. If this interview is all about the danger and the risk, then you can ask other people. I don't like your questions because you insist on certain subjects. There are many questions you could ask. You are obsessed.

You only appreciate the risk you have taken when you look back over your shoulder later on. I am retired from racing many years. I have to admit that when I consider the mileage I have done in motor racing and the time I have done it, from 1960 to 1992 – considering I have been able to do all sort of categories of sport, including motorcycle, including long-distance and Paris-Dakar – I have been many times flat out around this planet, and the mileage is probably incredible. Life is made of happiness and sadness because we will all die one day. The interesting thing is to do things through life.

Understand that – as you have to accept, the era was risky . . . so it means the drivers at the time needed a gentleman attitude because aggression could bring big trouble between you and another driver overtaking. There are no differences of having a goal. It's the basic attitude for everyone to aim to be the best and successful.

I don't think you need to be brave or have courage to do the things you like. Nobody forced you to do it, so no. In motor sport we were considered heroes at the time because the sport was very risky, because most of the people were accepting things as they were. Like us. We were accepting the risk. With time we get more intelligent and luckily we were surrounded by people who were also looking for a better time in motor sport. When you can compete in motor sport having a nice battle without having to pay for it, instead of these situations where you could have accidents.

## SUMMING UP

You think I am different. Actually, I don't have any personal ego of things I have done in the past. My surroundings where I live are not used to put my cups and trophies. The difference why? I don't know. But what is behind me is not part of my life today. I am very grateful for the good time I had but I believe all human life is very short – of that I am certain – and there are very many things to see and learn in life. Between my lovely childhood I had a fantastic time . . . It was a great life – the Jacky Ickx from yesterday has gone since a long time.

Luckily I am another person and my way of living today is not been like thirty to forty years ago. That's totally behind me and I am not interested in what is behind me. The people and the planet is much larger than only being interested in motor racing. It gave me a lot, but there is much more. Motor racing gave me a lot, but I see it pointless to find things just to satisfy my ego on something I have done a long, long time ago in my present life.

It gave me the chance to meet a lot of people and have memories of other people. It makes me realise that you can only achieve something good with the help of people around you – who will remain unknown – who are full of passion and motivation. These people who you meet and you like – whether it be Jackie or other people – these people exist, and from them you learn things and we have a luck in a way to be under the spotlight. But you cannot be under the spotlight if you do not realise that ninety per cent of the job is made by people who live in shadow. Then you have lost the point.

You had the opportunity of sailing the Atlantic. That's a real adventure when you are on your little boat in the middle of the ocean: definitely you don't feel important any more. It's fantastic. Then you have all your guides. Then you are very little. The same in the desert. You are very small. In the desert you have your feet in the sand. In the ocean you have your feet in the ocean and you will go far.

Simply because the paddock was open and you could see and talk to people without any difficulty, that time was very precious. In modern races there is no time for nothing. You don't see a driver. He goes from his motorhome to the car and back and nobody sees him. Even for you – if you want to have an interview [you wait] for two or three months and you will get five minutes.

That's already one hour. That's it. Thank you.

*Jacky then took us out for lunch.*

# 8
## JACKIE OLIVER

*Jackie was a fantastic interviewee as he tells it as it is and he has a great sense of humour. He also ended up running his own team, remains in management of the sport at a high level and therefore has a unique perspective. He also experienced – and was lucky to survive – some extremely dangerous accidents. Jackie still races to this day.*

There were lots of accidents during that period. A lot of guys died as a result. The cars were very dangerous, the fuel was contained without fuel bags, the safety of the circuits was poor – a very dangerous period, which I got through.

## ON JIM CLARK

At the Nürburgring, 1967 . . . opening practice lap, him [Jimmy] in his F1 car and me in my F2. Jimmy said, 'Follow me around and I'll show you a few tips.' So the first opening lap around the Nürburgring . . . I follow Jim Clark. I had already been there before so I knew the circuit. Knew the car. And then on the second lap he disappeared. I thought I was doing quite well until then.

He wasn't an icon. I never thought of him as, 'That's who I want to be' or, 'That's how successful I want to be.' I saw him as someone who was in the team and a lot better than me.

I got my opportunity in an F1 car to replace Jimmy [after he was killed]. I think I was a poor replacement. At the time I thought I was going to be the best but, looking back, I probably wasn't. Chapman had not only lost his best driver. He had lost his best mate.

## ON COLIN CHAPMAN

At Monaco Colin [gave me] some advice. He said, 'Lad, stay out of trouble – especially the first lap – and you will get your first championship point.' So with those words ringing in my ears I came out of the first tunnel in Monte Carlo into bright sunlight and there was Bruce McLaren and Cooper, and we had a bit of a tangle. It was either the harbour – you didn't have Armco barriers then [you would just go off into the water: frogmen in a rowing boat to rescue you] – or the rock face, going towards the chicane. I chose the rock face, but there was not enough room . . . so I took all the wheels off the Lotus.

Got back to the pits, Colin was sitting there with his charts and he looked down and said, 'You're fired.' He was a fantastic individual and I wasn't capable of coming up to his standards. But I didn't get much help and I made a lot of mistakes. I was a guinea pig for Colin. I have done more laps at Snetterton and Hethel than you can wave a stick at.

The things that used to break on Colin's cars were unbelievable. [They] used to test reliability and strength to see if it would break on the race track. There was not the technology you have now. The [Lotus] 49 . . . had an adjustable steering wheel, as Jimmy was a lot smaller than

Graham. He [Chapman] put one tube inside the other with a series of holes, so you could adjust the steering wheel. They put a 1B bolt in it, so when I got to the end of the straight first lap out . . . put the brakes on – remembering we did not have seat belts . . . put all the weight on the steering wheel . . . The bolt snapped, and I punched all the instruments with my knuckles.

## ON WINGS AND DOWNFORCE

Colin used to have these ideas. Never tested them. 'Let's stick it on the car.' So we turn up at races and have lots of practice going round the track. He turned up with wings on the back of Graham [Hill]'s car. And mine. Mine were very tall – right up. I think they got a round tube in the workshop and Colin said, 'I don't want it round, as it's got to be aerodynamic.' So they put it on rollers – flattened it. So mine was very tall – about 1.5 metres, with a wing on top – and Colin said, 'We've got to get it high to get it out of the turbulence.' This was before wind tunnels.

I looked at this, gave it a push, and it wobbled. So I asked, 'Is this all right?' Colin said, 'When you sit in an aeroplane the wings move. They have to be flexible.'

The first time I had driven a car with aerodynamics [wings] was at Rouen. The grip was unbelievable. The only trouble is that after about the fourth lap I moved over so I could pass the pits, and swapped lanes. As I swapped I lost control of the car. I don't know what happened – it went into a big slide. It's a kaleidoscope of colour. You really have no idea: you lose control and you are just a passenger . . . it happens that quickly. Opposite the pits there is a fantastic big chateau with the typical long gravel drive all the way up: wrought-iron gates in an abutment next to it.

I missed the wrought-iron gates. The rear of the car hit the abutment. Knocked the gearbox clean off the back of the car. I came out of the car – no seat belts – landed back in it . . .

The next thing I know Colin ran across the road saying, 'What happened?' I said, 'I don't know.' He said, 'Did you hit anything?' So I said, 'No,' as I thought the accident was my fault. He thought I might have hit something that had caused the accident. He ran back across the pits and said, 'The wings are pulling the gearboxes off the back of the engines.' He thought the gearbox had come off, which had caused me to lose control.

I think the turbulent air [as I overtook someone] . . . I think the wing bent the tubing, fell backwards – and as it fell backwards it picked the rear wheels off the ground. It was like riding a monoplane at 180 mph.

## ON CRASHING INTO JACKY ICKX AT THE SPANISH GRAND PRIX, 1970

I tried to steer to avoid all the people stopping for the hairpin. I steered across the track, caught Jacky Ickx full side on. [He was] leading the Spanish Grand Prix in the first lap. I T-boned him. All the fuel squirted out, got on to the exhaust pipe – and it went up in flames.

Whoosh. Big fireball. It exploded as soon as I hit. It was bright orange. I leapt out of the car like a gazelle, flames following me. Fortunately I did not run into anything. Jacky got out of the car and fell over, fell on the fuel on the ground – burnt the back of his legs, as his overalls acted like a candlewick. He still has the scarring, but we were lucky.

The only funny thing was – very dramatic – there was a very large Spanish marshal who had watched all of this, wide-eyed . . . saw this Englishman come sprinting out of this fireball, and I ran towards him. He looked at me, thinking, 'He's on fire,' and tried to take my helmet off without undoing the strap. So the only injury I had was a big bruise underneath my chin, where this stupid marshal had been swinging me around by my head.

## ON ONE OF THE GRAND PRIX DRIVERS' ASSOCIATION MEETINGS HE ATTENDED

There were boycotts everywhere. At the Belgian Grand Prix Jackie [Stewart] was calling a meeting because the circuit was not safe. Things had not been done that we wanted . . . we refused to practise. All on strike. All locked in this motorhome.

John Surtees by then had become a team owner and Mike Hailwood was driving for him. John was banging on the door, saying something like, 'Mike. If you don't come out you will not finish the season, and you are fired from my team for the rest of the year.'

And we are all inside – hanging on to him so he would not leave.

What a way to run a company.

## ON JOCHEN RINDT'S FATAL ACCIDENT

When a famous driver . . . appeared on a stretcher to a group of people that were first aid . . . They had Jochen Rindt. No one knew what to do. They were all standing round taking pictures and no one in control. I think it dawned on people that a particular individual had died at a racetrack because of complete incompetence.

It was a media circus with no competence, and as a result of the investigation afterwards someone said, 'Well, yeah. If you had done this, the guy would have lived.' He was leading the championship. He would have won the world championship and did, albeit posthumously. It's always a big impact with things like that.

## END NOTE

The sixties was a cracking time because the things that went on formulated the F1 we know today, both in safety and in commercialism.

I have gone through the whole phase. Started racing my father's car in the sixties. Turned pro in 67. I am as enthusiastic about it now as I was in my formative years.

The package we now have in F1 . . . some people say it's not as good as it used to be, and I say, 'Yes, it is.'

It is now a worldwide sport on TV with all the technical advantages . . . you can now see all the stuff that used to be hidden . . . it's fascinating.

# 9
# NINA RINDT

Jochen Rindt's wife

Jochen Rindt *Lockhard* ©2014

*Nina initially resisted doing an interview. I'd managed to persuade her that her story was really important. I explained that we hardly had any women and it was one of the most important elements of the story. She paints a vivid picture of what racing was like in this period – the excitement, the fashion and, of course, the ever-present danger. It's Nina and people like her that have to live with the consequences of poor safety from this period. I was very grateful that Nina agreed to do the interview.*

## ON JOCHEN

My father was a racing driver, so I went with him. My father raced against Jochen in 63, in Vienna and Hungary and Yugoslavia . . . Monza . . . We met later, skiing. My father introduced us, and that's how we met.

Jochen took me around a track in Finland which my father had built, and it was an open sports car – so I sat with the helmet on and I thought it was terrible. So frightening. And he said he didn't even go fast, so that's when I got a feel of how fast you can go. I wouldn't go again. He started calling me as I came to the race. I was living in Brussels, so I went with him to races for a while and we eventually got married in 1967.

It was a pretty good time for us. It was like a party all the time. You went from race to race, and dinners to parties. Great fun in the pits. We had a motorhome to sit in. That was great, but compared to today we were not spoiled at all. It was pretty rough, but fun. We talked together with the drivers – very good friends, a lot of them. Of course, there is always someone you don't like. But we had a great time, looking forward to the next race.

It wasn't really glamorous to be around the pits for hours on end day after day. You would just sit there waiting, as a woman. And you had to wait in such a way that it didn't make your husband nervous that you are waiting. But it wasn't glamorous. We saw a few good parties, if you call that glamorous. It was just party time – going to a race, a dinner and a dance. Life was organised for the drivers in those days.

We all had velvet suits and bright clothing, long skirts and scarves. We thought we were very smart but when you look at the photos . . . The hair was long, when you look at Jackie's hair – and Jochen had quite long hair, but not as long as Jackie. It looks awful. Not nice.

There is a lot of hanging around, especially for women – and then we would start doing the timings, so we were useful in some sense. It was pathetic. You had a stopwatch, and every time a car went past you clicked the stopwatch – and you had to deduct the timing so you knew exactly how every car did. You had it all in your book.

They wanted you to sit there and they would want to come in and find out how fast he was. It's not like that any more, is it? Jochen wanted me to be there as I wouldn't have seen very much of him otherwise – as he was driving F1, F2, 24 hours, Indy [Indianapolis]. There was one year he had fifty weekends. He was away all the time, every single weekend.

It's not like that any more.

Today it's all done by computers. We were the computers. It was quite fun. I don't know what year they started with computers, but I was gone. I wasn't there any more. When he died in 1970 they were still doing the timing – the wives, or whoever.

Jochen and I were driving in his little Mini with his van behind with his car and we stopped at a village in France and I asked, 'If you have a room to rent,' or a little hotel. He did everything himself. And then he would meet his mechanic down at the track who would help him ready the car. It was very amateurish. Great fun, though.

I was up on the podium in England when he won the English Grand Prix. It was fun. It was so exciting, because he was happy and he wanted to share it with me. So that was lovely. You remember these things from photographs.


He loved it. Absolutely loved it. It was like a love affair. But, of course – when a few of them died – it became a bit nerve-wracking for him, especially when it was close friends like Jim Clark and Piers Courage. So that wasn't very nice.

Once they sit in the car they forget and they just want to go fast – something they love. Like an obsession, yeah. The money wasn't big in those days . . . not big compared to today. Today you go into racing as it's a lot of money and it's exciting, but I don't know if it's the same passion.

The circuits and the cars were not really safe and the drivers didn't really care. There was nothing else, and they loved driving. That's the way it was: they went on and did it. Safety came in 67, starting with Jackie and Jochen going to circuits and checking them out. Didn't like this, didn't like that. Didn't think the cars were safe, in one aspect or another. Maybe because they had family and kids . . . I don't know.

He sort of nearly stopped in 70. Later, Piers died. I said, 'You can stop in the middle because a French driver stopped in the middle.' He said, 'I can't do that and I'm going to go on another year if I can become world champion.' . . . So he just wanted to [carry on]. After Piers's accident in June, when Jochen won the race and Piers died . . . we felt we were going from one funeral to the next. It was a bit drastic. I remember going to Piers's funeral dressed in black, taking an aeroplane to an F2 race and changing our clothes in the van at the circuit.

He just made sure that I knew about everything if he died, which I didn't want to talk about. Also, I had lived with my father – and he was an amateur, not a professional [racer] – and he was still alive, and – well, you don't think like that when you are young. You know about it, but you always think, 'It won't happen to me.'

When you have a child everything changes. You get a bit wary. It's like Bernie and Jochen had a little aeroplane they shared – flying from here to Monte Carlo for the Grand Prix – and they had a pilot for this flight. They said to the pilot, 'It's okay. We want to fly it, so you can sit in the back. Forget the airways. We go straight.' There was terrible turbulence – ice on the wings – and I was so angry, coming down in this. I said to Jochen, 'You want to kill yourself flying like that? I am flying back with Swissair,' and I went and booked my ticket back. He was always like that – the more dangerous the more fun.

If you had long flights you would go in the back and sleep. You don't do that today, and it was so much more expensive to travel then. But it was a joy to travel then. Today it's a nightmare. It was just a happy time going on a plane, eating and reading. No one had private planes in those days. Graham Hill had his own plane. Jochen and Bernie had [one]. No jets in those days – no money for those sorts of thing.

The paddock and the pits were open to everybody in those days. I think Bernie saw what a shambles it was and thought he could do something much better, which he did. So we would hide in the motorhome when it was at its worst.

## ON COLIN CHAPMAN AND DRIVING FOR LOTUS

I think Colin offered most money and it was the winning team, which is why he wanted to go there.

He always knew that Colin was very difficult – with building the cars – and a dangerous team, so to say. Colin had his opinion about things, but he [Jochen] said, 'Okay, I'm taking the chance.' He was trying to be persuaded to join McLaren. He had left Brabham because the car was not good and Lotus was the best car and he wanted to go with the best car. Then he saw how Colin was building the cars and he didn't like it, so there was constant arguments every race between them.

He had these cars that had wings. They flew in Barcelona instead of staying on the track . . . when the wing broke, you started flying. That's what happened to Jochen in Barcelona. He had a very bad accident. And then also the little tubes to the wheels – he had them hollow rather than stronger material because of the weight of the car. So that caused a big argument, as there was quite a lot of accidents.

He didn't care . . . the driver does as he is told, in his

opinion. He lost Jim Clark, who was his best driver, and he loved him dearly. So I don't think he had much time for drivers. If something happens there is a queue to take their place, so he didn't really care. But he was heavily criticised for this and later, after Monza, he built the car properly – but usually something has to go wrong before it's put right. We didn't socialise with him.

I remember Jochen wrote a letter to *Autosport*, which they published. But it was indirectly to Colin. I don't know whether he personally wrote to Colin. He wanted people to be aware of what was going on and try to make things safer. He couldn't discuss it with anyone. There was no organisation.

He just wanted to show Colin, 'I can tell the world what is going on.' [Colin] wanted a car which was quick and he didn't care if it wasn't that safe . . . this was the problem.

## ON JOCHEN'S ACCIDENT AT MONZA

Jochen said he refused to change to the Lotus 72, which was the new car. 'I will only drive the Lotus 49, and would you please bring it to Monza.' Colin could have said, 'If you don't want to drive it's up to you. But you are very close to the world championship so he felt put up against a wall. So we get to Monza and Colin said, 'The 49 is not here. You either drive the 72 or you don't,' so that was not very good.

Jochen's mood was okay – a bit angry with Colin – but he settled down, and going out in the car . . . I mean . . . just normal. If he was upset he didn't show it to me. That was it. So he went in the 72 and had the accident.

# UNBELIEVABLE

When he had his accident people came to me and said, 'He is all right. He is all right.' He was not, of course, but they would not let me into the ambulance and he was taken away, to work on him. There was a hospital transporter, but the law didn't allow that to be used. He had to be taken into hospital, which was ridiculous. Maybe he could have been saved. Who knows? But by the time he got to hospital it was too late. My father came to meet me with Sally Courage, so we looked after each other this time.

And then Colin felt really bad. He immediately left the country in his own small plane and dropped me in Geneva. Colin didn't really care. He cared after the accident because he was charged with manslaughter in Italy, but not in England. So he could not go back for a while.

I didn't like him because he wouldn't do what Jochen wanted. Emerson took his place, and why not? Jochen would have done the same. Emerson is a very nice guy.

I was very angry that the world could go on when he had to die but I think that is a normal feeling. Emotions are emotions. He did what he loved doing and you can't argue with that. We did have a good time. I am sure he loved every minute of his driving.

## ON JOCHEN BECOMING THE FIRST POSTHUMOUS WORLD CHAMPION

It was nice they gave it to him, as that was what he always wanted. But it was very sad he never knew. The trophy is there [she points to the bookshelf]. I went to pick it up for him. I couldn't face all that. It was awful, for a long time. I still get not too happy talking about it, or watch a film about him. Life goes on, and I have a daughter. She misses a lot not to have a father but there are lots in that position, or worse. She worked in F1 for four years and she tried to understand the whole world of motor racing, and I think she did.

I didn't think Jochen had an ego but maybe that's because I was close to him. With the public he was very good. He would do anything . . . autographs . . . nothing was too much. If there was some event in Austria he would go and help them for free, just to be nice. He was very friendly with strangers, which sometimes annoyed me. I would want to go home and he would stop and talk. But there is a lot of ego in motor racing and lots of people think they are somehow amazing because they are in motor racing . . . they think there is no other world apart from theirs.

There is more to life than just motor racing. He was very special to me, but why I loved him? It's difficult. You never know why you love someone. You either love them or you don't. He was a very generous, kind man. He said, 'I always put myself in someone else's shoes first, before I make a decision.' He was very young to have that attitude – mature for his age. Maybe it's because he didn't have any parents. He was brought up by his grandparents.

We were always going somewhere. We had to be on time, but basically I have very good memories. It was a lot of fun. We certainly had a lot of fun.

# *10*
# EMERSON FITTIPALDI

Emerson Fittipaldi *Lowland* © 2014

*Interviewing Emerson Fittipaldi was a special moment in the whole of the Killer Years production. To this day I remember his warmth – his smile. He has an aura about him that stays with you – a presence.*

*As we parted he said, 'Thank you, John. That was the most amazing interview I have ever had.'*

## ON BEING THE BEST AND ON RACING

I always say that when you think you are the best, you start to lose.You always have ground to improve. Look at any athlete – any sport. It's a constant improvement of yourself, your dedication, your effort, your passion for the sport – and I always wanted to improve. Learning more one mile in a racing car is always something new. You never have enough experience. I was lucky to be able to race for thirty years internationally and was always learning. Even in my last race I was learning more and more.

I loved racing, even to my last speedway – and I had a crash. I still loved every mile I have done. I still love driving. I think the excitement to be driving by yourself – and just the challenge for you to put in a quick lap – is a fantastic feeling. The feeling of going into the corner, sliding the car, drifting, controlling, braking on the limit – and then, when you are competing against each other, and the adrenalin . . . I think it's incredible, as I have loved the sport since I was five years old.

## ON BECOMING WORLD CHAMPION

It's not just that day, it's the weekend. Arriving in Italy on the Thursday . . . and I was sleeping, and Peter – the manager – he called me and said, 'Do you speak Italian?' The transporter crashed just before Milan, and that was the start of the disaster weekend. My racing car was upside down with spare parts all over the place. So we immediately called England to bring the spare car. That's how we started the weekend championship in Monza.

On race day we were driving the spare car, and later – in warm-up – the fuel tank is leaking. They have to take off the fuel tank – fuel cell. Replace it. The car was ready just a few minutes before going to the grid. So much pressure. When the race started it all went perfect. To win the championship, to win the Grand Prix on the same day is the best you can achieve – and the last few laps I remember, 'I'm going to be world champion. I'm going to be world champion!' and it lasted. It was the longest lap of my laps. [When] I left Brazil and my dream was to be a Grand Prix driver . . . I was not even thinking about being world champion and I was very lucky and blessed. From 1969 to 72 I was the reigning world champion. That was amazing. That day in Monza I will never forget.

Everything happened so fast. I was on the podium with the Brazilian flag. My father was doing a broadcast for the Brazilian radio and it was very emotional – a father interviewing his son, the Brazilian world champion. And then I was living in Switzerland and we had a big party at the Brazilian Embassy. That night at 4 a.m. I drove back to Switzerland and arrived at 7 a.m. in the morning in Lucerne, where I used to live – the French part of Switzerland – and I stop at the traffic lights and there was a news-stand and I read on the newspaper: *Fittipaldi Champion du Monde!* That was unbelievable to see. That was me. That was the first I realised, looking on the news, that I was world champion.

Inside you are still the same, but around you things change. Circumstances change. It was tremendous pressure on me – from the Brazilian press, from the sponsors, from Colin [Chapman], from Lotus. It was very difficult. It's always nice. Then, when you win, you have to be performing because everybody expects and that's how we say the top athlete that can stay on high performance all the time is the real champion. It's very difficult to be there.


## ON DRIVING FOR LOTUS

The best car I drove in my racing career was the Lotus 72, because it was a car I could talk to and it would talk to me. We loved each other and it was an incredible relationship. I knew everything from the car. I raced the chassis number five for four years. It was an incredible car – the most consistent car that I ever raced in my career.

Well, it was hard – but at that time we always accepted the risk of motor racing. It was a high-risk mid-sixties to seventies but to me it was the best opportunity I could have in my life – to have Colin Chapman ask me to drive. My first invitation to drive Formula One was Frank Williams, when I was still driving F3 in England. He asked me to drive for his team. He was making a new team – he had Piers Courage, who died in a crash, and he asked me to replace Piers. At the same time Colin called me, and I was driving F3 semi-works car – Lotus. Then, I remember, I walk in Colin's office in Norwich. My legs were shaking. Colin Chapman inviting me to drive was like a dream. I accepted immediately, with all the history of Lotus – Jim Clark, Jochen Rindt. He wanted me to start at the beginning of the season – 1970 – but I told Colin that I need another four months in F2 before I can drive in F1. Then I wait to July to start.

## ON COLIN CHAPMAN

Colin was extremely competitive. He had intuition – how to get the car going really fast. 'How can I improve the car? What am I missing? What can I do for tomorrow?' I would finish a practice Friday afternoon. At night I would have dinner with Colin and we would describe what the car was doing on various parts of the track. Colin would go back to the garage to change the whole car. Saturday morning the car was fast. He had this perception . . . basic instinct on how to improve a car, like intuition. He put a hand here . . . start moving this – and I knew something good was going to come out.

He was a genius. A lot of energy inside, calling. He wanted to win races – and, with his engineering background – his ideas always relate to dynamic, very light cars . . . extremely resistant. That's why we had so many mechanical failures – but he was inside, calling. He was a great human being. In 72, after I won my first world championship – he had lost Jimmy, then Jochen – Jimmy Clark was very close to him – and one day he come to me ... 'Emerson, I like you very much – but I don't want to get too close to you. I have great loss that I don't want to happen again.' People saw that Colin was not taking care of his drivers. Colin was worried about his drivers, like any human being would, but the impact when he lost Jimmy was devastating for him.

I don't know the reputation of the mechanical failures of the Lotus history had, but behind that failing Colin had his heart to the drivers. He liked the drivers. I had a one-to-one relationship with Colin. At that time we didn't have computers, electronics. There was just the driver/engineer or the driver/team manager, and Colin was a bit of everything. He was the owner, the engineer, the technical head guy for the team – which is why this relationship was very important. He was a very strong human being. Colin was always afraid something was going to happen to his driver, for sure.

## ON CRASHING

I had a few mechanical failures. One was the turbine car, and I broke a front wheel in Zandvoort in the Lotus 72. A huge crash: one of my worst. I was very lucky. But it was wheel failure, and the wheel was made outside Lotus. I don't know if the design of the wheel was too marginal or if the wheel was already fatigued or old. It's hard to say. But it was a really bad mechanical failure. The front of the car was completely off. My foot was stuck: it broke the fuel tank. I was lucky. I nearly broke my foot, but I couldn't get out of the car. This was in practice. I hit the Armco. I went up in the air, and spinning ... and the front of the Lotus ... I think, 'This thing is going to blow [up],' because there is a lot of fire, and I couldn't get out. Graham Hill – he stopped and got out of his car to help me get out . . . the marshal, who are not trained . . . and then Graham asked the crew to get a saw, and Graham . . . after twenty minutes Graham got me out . . . We were still missing the professional team on a crash like that.

In 72 – the first Brazilian Grand Prix – I am leading the race for Lotus – first time in Brazil, and second is the Brabham. There is a ramp and I am in fifth gear – very fast – and there is a kink. The rear suspension gets a load, and as I go to the kink – the left – the wishbone collapses. The rear wheel turns and I spin and I go backwards into the pit full speed. I stop there, and an English journalist said, 'Excellent car control.'

## ON JOCHEN RINDT'S AND FRANÇOIS CEVERT'S ACCIDENTS

On the Saturday morning I had breakfast with Jochen, and he was tired from doing so much [setting up his own team – Emerson was to be a member] . . . there was his team, and Bernie Ecclestone. They were partners in 1971 . . . Two hours later he was killed. For me it was a disaster. It was only my fourth Grand Prix and my teammate was dead. For me, very difficult.

He was a natural driver. He was very German, very conservative – but very nice person. When you knew Jochen, you liked Jochen. Very clever. He was the best in F2 at the time. He was winning everything. Jochen had always been extremely good to me because my first F1 testing at Silverstone with the Lotus 49, Colin asked him to drive to do a few laps. He did a few laps before me and he came out and said, 'The car is ready for Emerson,' and I start first time ever in Grand Prix car. After three laps Jochen is given me the sign. He wants me to do well. He was like a mentor to me. When I stopped he and Colin came to get my comments and I told Colin, 'It's too understeering,' and Jochen had just driven the car before and Jochen said, 'Emerson, the car is not understeering. Just use more throttle.' And he was right.

After he was killed I went home. I knew it was tough to race. Every time I left home with the bag with the helmet in I thought, 'Sunday, am I coming back here?' But when I arrived at the race track I never thought about that. My mind was to go racing to win. It was my dream to be there. I was never thinking that was going to happen to me and there was a type of commitment.

Jochen's crash was so close and so very real. I knew it could happen to me and I was lucky. I lost so many good friends. There was a lot of friendship and respect between the drivers – different from now – and you look at the picture at the beginning of the season . . . twenty-one drivers, and there were three who were not going to be there. The odds were 7/1 to survive.

One of the worst I had was with François [Cevert] in 1973. I was fifteen seconds behind and I saw the yellow flag going to the fast corners in Watkins Glen. I said it is bad because it is fast, and I slow down the Lotus. And then I saw the rear wing of the car sticking out from the Armco . . . the rest of the car under the Armco. I stopped. As my experience from Holland, I knew the marshals were volunteers – not trained. It was a disaster that I saw. I drove the Lotus back to the pits. I told my wife and I told Colin, 'I don't want to talk to anyone.'

The only place where I could be by myself was in the parking lot in Watkins Glen, and asking God, 'Should I still continue? I love this sport, but should I still continue? Something is wrong in this sport.' I remember I was in the parking lot for an hour and a half by myself. I cried a lot. I asked, 'Should I continue, or not?' And then I heard the loudspeaker from F1 practice was going to restart again. Two hours later I was going by the place where François just got killed and I thought, 'This is not correct. Something is wrong.'

François was close to me, as we started racing from together – and he was a very happy, very special person. François and . . . like Ronnie [Peterson] . . . losing one after the other, I asked the question, 'Should I continue?' Jackie Stewart had just retired, at that Grand Prix.

## ON THE GRAND PRIX DRIVERS' ASSOCIATION

I used to do track inspections – to look at the Armco, to see how it could be improved. I did a lot of track inspections in Holland, Belgium. The worst experience I had was the Spanish Grand Prix. I was the defending world champion for McLaren. I used to jog on the Thursday before the race and I saw wiring holding the Armco with bolts and washers, and I ask the organiser, 'See this? This is wrong. This is a street circuit.' 'It will be ready,' he says. It never happened Friday . . . the same, Saturday . . . the same, Sunday. Then I went to my sponsor and said, 'I refuse to race tomorrow. There is enough risk to motor sport, but I cannot accept the track that is not prepared for a Grand Prix. A street circuit with Armco with wiring. You kick it and it would fall down.'

And then the organiser said, 'If you don't start we are going to impound the McLaren.' I was the world champion, so I told the sponsor [I was not happy] and they released me . . . and I went home to Geneva. As I landed in Geneva the Swiss TV is waiting for me and I didn't know what happened at the Grand Prix. They tell me there has been a big crash at the Grand Prix. Five people have been killed.

I was revolted . . . it was a disaster, and we knew it was going to happen. That's exactly the fight you have to improve the tracks. At the same time the FIA suspended me. I didn't know this, but when I caught the plane they suspended me because I didn't continue the race. The Brazilian representative for the FIA told me two months later. And then they unsuspended me after the crash.

## ON TRYING TO STAY SAFE

I hired a doctor to go to every Grand Prix with me. He had a survival kit, which they didn't have at the track – and it was very difficult for me to arrive with a Swiss doctor who has to go to the local doctor and say, 'I am Emerson Fittipaldi's doctor, and I am here in case anything happens to him.' But that was illustrating that most of the countries were not prepared. Even in the ambulance they had nothing inside – a nurse, but not even a doctor. I had to write a letter authorising, for example, if I had a bad burn he had to take me to Germany. He had power of attorney from me to be able – before my family – to take a decision on my behalf if I was brain-damaged. I had everything organised. It was very expensive for me to take this doctor all over the Grand Prix but I felt much safer. The following year I made a pool with myself and Carlos Reutemann . . . we shared the doctor: he was looking after three drivers.

## EMERSON'S FINAL WORDS

We always need idols. I think people need idols to give you inspiration of life. I had Fangio as my idol – another Brazilian driver [Fittipaldi means South American here]. I remember first time I arrive in Brands Hatch – 1969. I saw people giving autographs who were my idols and I was standing in line to ask for them. Then a year later I was racing against them.

I always say the best teacher is not the one that teaches, but the one that inspires you. The best psychologist I know is God.

# 11
# BEN HUISMAN

*Ben was Clerk of the Course at Zandvoort, Holland, where Roger Williamson had his fatal accident. He describes that day in candid detail. His story is interesting, as he was in charge when there was a fatality – and prior to that he also had to meet Jackie Stewart, who was trying to make the track safer. Ben has had to live with this experience, and openly shares what that is like.*

We didn't believe Jackie Stewart . . . that we built the circuit . . . we had spent a lot of money on it, and he came and said, 'It's not yet up to the standard.'

I was so convinced that everything was great – that it was a waste of time. The track was great. It was accepted by the FIA in Paris, so what is he coming to do?

Over the years we realised that he was right. Not because of the accident of Roger Williamson – but later on you find out that he was right, and that safety really did matter. Fortunately we can say that after many years we rebuilt this circuit. We made it after the recommendations – made it safer, and we kept it safer – and it has probably saved the lives of a lot of drivers who have been racing here.

If you see those pictures and films of the sixties you see the straw bales around the tower, and you did not realise how dangerous it was – and you accepted that. It has changed completely, and the attitude to motor racing and the possibility of an accident has changed so much. So, over the sixties and seventies, it changed.

I had to pick him [Jackie Stewart] up from the airport. He was a celebrity then, and he also thought of himself as a celebrity. Nice guy, but he knew it – so he did not come through the VIP exit, as you have to arrange that . . . as I had to keep him down to earth, and he hated that. He hated having to sit in the car with another driver and I had to drive my orange BMW 1800 Ti. I drove twenty-five kilometres per hour from the airport to Zandvoort. I had only done this once, with my father, in the dark. We never spoke a word in the car. I drove twenty-five kilometres an hour and nothing, so that was not a very good start for the relationship between the F1 driver and the organiser. I think, 'Very stupid of me, doing that.'

We rebuilt the circuit according to his plans. We had [already] rebuilt the circuit, but you can imagine that – the FIA – they also had to have a say in it, and they wanted to check the circuit for themselves – and Jackie Stewart came over. We invited Graham Hill, and he was a friend, but he looked in another way. Jackie looked mainly for the safety: Graham came more for the promotion of the Grand Prix in Zandvoort.

Jackie came for the safety and we went over budget. It was quite a lot of money and in the end we went bankrupt because we couldn't afford the interest, and so on. So for us it was not a question of safety. It was a question of money. We had to build to the FIA ideas. We had guard rails, we had this and that, and Jackie came up with more things we had to install. We had to install more guard rails and fences, I think.

About two and a half million pounds . . . we had to raise that from the industry, from the government, from the state bank. It wouldn't be allowed any more, now – but we got it, and we were building our dream and saving car racing in Holland, because the circuit was out of the question. It was a total loss. The grass had grown through the asphalt, the clipping points were bushes – so [we did it] to save motor racing. As a club we came up with the idea of, 'Let's buy it. Let's buy the circuit.' So we went to the community and they said, 'You can't buy it.' So we said, 'We want it, so give it to us because we want to have motor racing.' It was crazy. The opposition was terrible, but we got the money from left and right. We made shares and God knows what, but we got the money – and by the time it was ready the cash box was empty. And then came Jackie Stewart, who said, 'It's not good. You have to move things here and there.' So I can't say we were on speaking terms.

We rented it for fifty years, which is a long time when you are young. I was in my thirties, so we had a wonderful thing with the tower – and the pit boxes, the grandstand . . . 80,000 people on the first race – so I thought I must go on.

The main thing was we had to rebuild the circuit before 1973 and we could have the Grand Prix back. It was important because it was the future of racing. And that is the thing that I am still proud of, and we have done it – with the help of others, of course. We have saved racing in Holland.

The only problem is on a day like today when it's windy and there is a lot of sand on the track. So on a race today – or a practice today and a race tomorrow – is completely different, as all this sand blows on it. But as a safe circuit . . . yes. We sold it as a safe circuit and, according to the time, it was what Jackie wanted. It was a lot of things he wanted changed and it was also a lot of money. And that was the point, as I thought, 'What a lot of work we have to do again.'

But of course the end result was that it was not safe. But, more importantly, the safety measures – not the track, but off the track – were of that period. I was just wondering about telephones I was using this morning. This thing is quite easy. [Then] you had to wind it and then you had the telephone – it was like an ex-army thing.

And if the wires broke you did not have any connection with the posts along the track – and if you think about that today, it was incredible. But that was the time. That was one of the things that changed very quickly after 73-74, and you have safety cars and so on. If you look back it's always easy, but it was as it was.

It's a fantastic track. The F1 drivers – they liked it. They liked Zandvoort. If they came here they [brought] the family here, because it was something great. The track so near to the beach, the village – and they liked the track itself. One of the few drivers that didn't like it all was Jackie Stewart. With most of the other drivers – Hunt, etc. – they liked it, and maybe also because Amsterdam was close by.

It's a special place. I walked around it quite a lot of times. Grands Prix nowadays are like concentration camps. I think in the sixties and seventies you could touch the drivers and the cars, it was so close. Scrutineering was in the garage in the village and they drove over the streets from Zandvoort, and the villagers ran to the track. Impossible nowadays, but it made it much more interesting.

I was the Clerk of the Course. I like organisations where one man is the boss, and I don't like organisations where you have a board and you have to discuss everything. I was the boss and that was it. The good thing is if it's a success you get it and if it's a failure you get it, but it's much easier and it's always the way I have run businesses.

It was just like any other business – the organisation itself. You have so many decisions, and we were used to running races. We were organising all the sports car races and touring car races – so the same organisation, but just a bit bigger for the Grand Prix. And at the end of the race we had the prize-giving, and all the drivers and team managers came and got their envelope with the money in it.

We had a house here in Zandvoort because I had four little children, and we drove to Zandvoort in the morning and we saw the crowds – 80,000 people. And we were so happy because it had cost a lot of money, so with 80,000 people we knew how much money had come in. It's always a gamble. If it starts raining you get half of that, so we were happy. One night we were driving a motorbike around the track and we saw all the dunes filled with people and . . . on top of the world.

Nothing could go wrong. The weather was nice, the spectators were there, the racing cars were on the grid. We got a beautiful cup from the Royal Automobile Club for all the work we had been doing. Fantastic. That was the feeling of the morning, and everyone said, 'Fantastic, Ben. You have done it.' Success has a lot of friends, as you can imagine. Top of the bill. It was a good atmosphere.

I was at the starting line, as that was my job. I was the Clerk of the Course, so I really don't remember how the start went. But I was there and it was [a] good start, as I have a trick that probably others have. If you look at the starting grid . . . there were no lights in those days, so you would be looking at the drivers and they would be looking at you – and as long as you did not blink your eyes they all think you are looking especially at him. So they don't move the car until the flag drops, and if you blink they take advantage of that. So we had a good start.

We were all in a good mood and we were all in a single ship. It was like building the *Titanic*. Nothing could go wrong. It was a new track with everything in and on it and a very good start, and 80,000 people. Everybody was happy. Maybe the guy at the back of the grid not so happy.

After eight laps – when Roger Williamson went off and got killed – we didn't hear that. I got all reports at home, but I'm not interested in rereading it. We didn't know. Communications were very bad – and the only reason I decided not to stop the race was that the lap times were still the same, so we thought, 'There can't be anything on the track.'

Then we got the message that the guy was standing next to the car, and it was burning. Another reason was: if we stop it we can never get the race restarted – with 80,000 people. So I took the gamble and the risk and said, 'We continue.' And, of course, the big impact was on television. But we didn't have television. It was broadcast, so that people at home knew more than we did.

Communication between the person on the track and communication centre? Almost non-existent. As I told you, it was a telephone – and then, people had broken lines, because there were just telephone lines laying in the sand. The safety cars, the fire brigade, was not up to standard – but, again, my responsibility. I thought the fire trucks were up to the standard and they were not. If you look back they should have had this and that and they didn't, but the track was up to standard.

So it was the first of those things that was live on TV, and this case with Roger – it was an impact. They said the *Titanic* was unsinkable but it still went down, so that was more or less the end of my career. As you are hit, you can't function any more. So I accepted that.

This particular thing . . . I would say that over the years it comes back, I don't know why, probably because you get older . . . but when I was racing as an amateur and I had lost friends I realised much later that I never thought about their wife, their children. It happened. We had the funeral and that was it, and we said, 'Stupid accident.'

The impact of Roger Williamson was bigger because you could see it on the television again and again – and, of course, the impact was made in the racing world. But over the years you are busy, you have your family. Racing goes on, and then it comes back.

But you have to go on with your life. It seems ridiculous, but I let my sons eat as much as possible so they could eat themselves out of an F1 car if they got too big. So they never raced single seaters. They race sports cars and touring cars.

I have always said, 'It's my fault. I didn't give the guy a way to escape it – a chance to survive it. I have not killed him – that's nonsense – but I haven't given him a chance to survive,' and other people say, 'Ben, you shouldn't say that. It's nonsense.' But it's what I feel. I didn't give him that chance to survive. We rebuilt the track again and again, and I can say that I saved a lot of other people's lives – otherwise we would all be crippled to death. But you can't count them. It's a question of responsibility for me and I have always taken my responsibility.

There is not much difference between success and failure, and you can never know what to expect in life. We have to go and look at the bright side – and that's most important, and that's what I do. So I think I look quite young for seventy-four, and that's because I look on the bright side.

# *12*

# JACQUI HAMILTON

Roger Williamson's girlfriend when he died

Roger Williamson *Lowland* © 2014

*This interview is pretty much complete – I wanted it left as it was because Roger died and this gives an intimate insight into what he was like and helps preserve his memory. It also shows the effects of the lack of safety in a poignant way that should never be forgotten.*

Ian Phillips introduced me to Roger, and Roger and I hit it off. Funny and sweet. Not my type at all. But he was just a nice guy – looked rather nice, had a twinkle in his eye – and I thought, 'I quite like you.' The third day, 'I'm off to Brazil. Will you come with me?' and I said, 'Excuse me. I have a company to run. I can't just up and leave.' He said, 'I don't care. I want you to come.'

Needless to say I didn't go, and I wish I had. It was one of these things . . . when you think, 'God, I wish I had been there. And when he got back from Brazil he phoned me and said he wanted to see me again – can he see me? I said, 'Yes, of course,' and from that moment onwards we just hit it off.

I was living with my parents at the time. He had just bought a house in Leicester, and my parents were in Bedford – even though my business was in London – and we were going back and forward and I started going to races with him, and that went on until he actually died in Zandvoort.

There was a lot of things I liked about him . . . he used to take me to all the circuits, and he used to get in his own car and we used to drive around at ten miles an hour, increasing it every lap by ten miles until we got to the skin of the teeth . . . and thinking, 'Oh, my God.' But his hands were very reassuring. They were so sexy. It was one of those little things that made me really fancy him. We were so opposite. We both came from completely different backgrounds, and in that way it made it more fun.

He never drank, or very rarely – and I always drank, and we would go out for dinner and he would say, 'I suppose you want some of that red stuff.' He says, 'You choose. I don't know what I'm doing,' and I say, 'Yeah, but you have to try a little bit. You have to educate yourself into wine.' From that moment onwards we had a very comfortable but sexy relationship – and it sounds daft – but one of the things . . . when we got to Zandvoort it was freezing, and I said, 'I am going to freeze to death at that circuit.' So he said, 'Here is some money. Go and buy yourself a coat.' I still have the money because I never bought the coat.

People asked, 'Would you ever have got married . . . was he the love of your life?', because we never argued, and nothing went wrong in the relationship. I mean . . . we were only together about a year, so everything was idyllic – and it remains in my mind as an idyllic relationship. My husband would not be happy for me to say that but I just think that he was a personality and he was one of these people that was totally and utterly determined. I suppose the thing I remember most was his determination to win – and he had the killer instinct, which I think you have to have. And he had it.

Roger was going to make it and he was going to be up there and I think people would have put their money where their mouth was to make sure that he got the cars that he would need to become world champion.

When his friend Gerry got killed . . . and all the drivers were up in arms, because the circuit was so dangerous, and they said, 'Right. We are not going to race.' They all had a meeting with the officials and Roger said, 'I don't care if I am the only one on that grid. I am starting that race.' And that was him being absolutely determined. The race did go ahead in the end, but he just wanted to win no matter what – and that was another thing that was attractive. Powerful men, even if they are as ugly as sin . . . the power is actually attractive, and he had that sort of charisma. He was going to win, no matter what, and I believe he would have been a world champion. I am absolutely positive.

He had such a good relationship with Tom Wheatcroft – who helped him so much in the beginning, as Roger had no money. He was there with his father Dodger – and Dodger was another character who didn't like women at all. It didn't matter who they were: they were getting in the way of Roger racing – and he didn't know how to take me, as Dodger was quite short and I am quite tall – and I wasn't the type of person that Roger usually went out with.

His attitude was, 'I'm not sure about her.' Then he came round and realised that we were an item and that we were happy and that I was making Roger happy – and I wasn't getting in the way of the racing, because I liked the racing. I liked being there. I liked watching it. I wasn't very good with the timer, but I did try my best. And we had such fun. We used to go in the transporter over to France. The transporter was not the most glamorous of transporters . . . I just wished it hadn't stopped.

I speak dodgy French and we hadn't booked any rooms,

so Roger and Tom said, 'You go and organise the bed.' I said, 'Okay' – so we ended up in some very strange hotels, I hasten to add – and that was half the fun. We had a little moped thing, which I had never driven before – so they said, 'You go off and get some food.'

So I am on this little moped thing, that I probably shouldn't have been driving – and it was just that sort of thing . . . there was great camaraderie among everybody. It's competitive on the track, because the money wasn't there – and people were managing to race, having got a car from scrap. Obviously, a bit later on, when Roger was driving Marches and things, it wasn't quite as bad as when he first started – but everybody seemed to get on with everybody else. There was not that rivalry that there is now.

## ON ROGER WILLIAMSON'S CRASH AT ZANDVOORT

All I can remember is going to the circuit with Roger. We had had a quiet night out the night before. I had my wine . . . he was very laid back, very straight. He always had to have the period before the race where he didn't want to talk to anybody – just wanted to reflect. So he had gone to do his reflection, as it were . . .

It was a beautiful sunny day, and I guess the one thing I was thinking was that we had actually talked about getting engaged, and he said, 'We have two or three races to go. After that we will go and look for an engagement ring.' I didn't particularly want a ring – it's not really me – but he said, 'We will talk about it later,' so that was sort of on my mind . . .

Then I went down to the pits and thought, 'I am not going to see much of the race from there,' and thought I would rather watch it on the television. So I sat and watched it on the TV, and Roger was doing well. He was never going to win, and I'm sitting there watching it – and someone said there had been an accident. Couldn't really see anything, just a pile of smoke on the screen, so no one knew anything and no one said anything. So I thought, 'What's going on?' I went down to the pits and by that time they had found out it was Roger. I went absolutely numb and I thought, 'No. No, not Roger,' as the one thing he had always said all his life . . . 'I don't ever want to be burnt alive,' – which is what happened to him.

If he had been rescued earlier he would have lived. He hadn't broken anything, either. All I can remember is being shoved into a car – taken straight to the airport. I don't remember it, but I was put in first class and they said they would not have anyone sitting next to me. And someone got hold of my father – so when I got to Heathrow my father was there with my old boyfriend, who was still a great mate. They took me home. No one would let me see a paper for three days, as it was a three-day wonder and everything was in the paper. I still didn't believe it. I thought I was dreaming it, as it was the one thing he didn't want to have happen to him – and that made it worse for me, because he was burnt.

I saw David [Purley, who tried in vain to save Roger's life] at the funeral – and we chatted, and I said, 'I am just so proud of you for trying to do . . .' I mean . . . really, he shouldn't have been trying to do something. I just think he was really, really brave, as he could have been burnt as well. He was very sweet, very kind, very charming – but I didn't see him after that.

I don't know very much about the whole thing – but it just

seemed that the marshals didn't have any protective clothing on, so how could they get near the car? They had a little tabard thing on saying, 'We are a marshal,' but there was no fire extinguishers. It was only David who had a fire extinguisher in his car who tried to put the flames out – and, okay – we now know the barriers weren't secured properly. They were just secured in the sand, rather than being concreted in – and also the fact that the fire engine wasn't allowed to cross the track and it had to go all the way round, and it was virtually opposite from where he crashed. So I feel very bitter about that.

Of course we had the memorial service, where they unveiled this really nice statue at Donington – and that was the last time I saw Tom, and it wasn't long after that he died. It was nice that he had been remembered in the Donington museum – for Roger – which I couldn't go and look at. It was the one thing I couldn't do, but I have very fond memories – and this sounds really stupid – but so like him. I suppose the other thing that was quite quirky about Roger was that he felt you had to have a gimmick, like other people do – and his gimmick was his hat. He went everywhere with this hat. He would take it off to put his helmet on, and when he took his helmet off he put his hat back on again.

If he put it down somewhere and couldn't find it he would go ballistic . . . it was his lucky charm – and it suited him, actually – so there were lots of things like that that made him the person that he was.

One of my great joys was that I did go to Monaco with Roger and . . . it was a good time. We had a laugh. Mind you, he kept saying, 'It's so expensive,' but even in those days it was expensive. But it was fun. It was lovely. All the drivers were friendly towards everybody. Now they don't smile. You see them being interviewed and you think, 'A little smile would be quite nice. Let's see some of your personality.'

I went to races afterwards, but it wasn't quite the same.